Explore
MY PATH

THIS GUIDE BELONGS TO:

_____

Explore My Path
Career Resource Guide
Compiled and Presented by Reginald C. Bean

Designed, produced, and published by
SPARK Publications
SPARKpublications.com
Charlotte, North Carolina

Stock Image Credit: Borderline Artistic / Spiral Media / Visual Generation / Shutterstock.com

Printed in the United States of America

Paperback, March 2025, ISBN: 978-1-953555-83-0
Library of Congress Control Number: 2025902803

TO THOSE STARTING OUT IN LIFE

Life's a game where action is what drives change. You can't just believe in something—you've got to put in the work to make it real. Growth comes when you own your choices, learn from missteps, and stay committed to your dreams. Real strength isn't about showing off; it's about staying true to yourself and doing the right thing, even when no one's watching. When you help others and approach life with an open heart, you'll find your purpose and your power. We're all in this together, and when we support each other and keep the faith, we all rise.

YOU CAN VISIT US FOR ADDITIONAL RESOURCES OR TO PROVIDE FEEDBACK.

exploremypath.com

getstarted@exploremypath.com

TABLE OF CONTENTS

CAREER PATHWAYS

HOW TO USE THIS GUIDE

A simple way to explore your path

So, you've got your hands on a shiny new career guide, and you're probably wondering how to make the most of it. Don't worry, it's easier than you think! This guide is like your GPS, helping you navigate the incredible career pathways available to you. Whether you dream of jumping straight into a job after high school or you're planning to hit the books in college, this guide is here to help you figure it out. Let's dive in!

STEP 1:
Get to Know Your Guide
First, let's take a quick tour of your career guide. Think of it like the map of an amusement park. Each section is a different ride (or career pathway), with a little intro to excite you and details on what you'll need to do to get on board. You'll find info on the skills and abilities you'll pick up and what jobs you can land if you choose that path. Once familiar with the layout, you'll quickly zoom through the guide, but don't forget to take notes along the journey.

STEP 2:
What Do You Like?
Next up: Time for some self-reflection. What gets you excited? What subjects do you enjoy? Maybe you love tinkering with gadgets or you're the one everyone goes to for advice. Consider what you love doing—this will help you zero in on the pathways that suit you best.

STEP 3:
Check Out the Pathways
Now that you've got a better idea of what makes you tick, it's time to explore. Flip through the guide and check out the different pathways that match your interests. Each one will give you the lowdown on the courses you'll need to take, the skills you'll develop, and what kind of future awaits you. It's like browsing favorite playlist—everything sounds good, but which song is calling your name for that weekend workout?

STEP 4:
Plan Your Journey
Alright, now that you've picked a pathway (or two), it's time to map out your journey. Use the guide to plan your classes for the next few years. Think of it like planning a road trip—plot out the stops (or courses) you need to hit to reach your destination. And don't forget to chat with your school counselor; they're like your trusty copilot, helping you stay on course.

STEP 5:
Keep It Flexible
Remember, life is full of surprises, and your interests might change as you go. It's okay! Revisit your career guide now and then to see if something new catches your eye or if you need to tweak your plan. Think of your career journey like a playlist—you can always shuffle things around to keep it fresh and fun.

And there you have it! With this simple, step-by-step approach, you'll make the most of your career guide quickly. Here's to finding a path that's as exciting and unique as you are!

Ready to get started?

Scan the QR code and answer a few questions to explore your career interests.

WHAT IS WORK-BASED LEARNING

A Real-World Head Start for Your Future Career

Work-Based Learning (WBL) and Career & Technical Education (CTE) work together to give students a powerful, real-world introduction to future careers. CTE programs build technical knowledge and hands-on skills through classroom instruction, labs, and career-focused coursework, while WBL takes that learning a step further by directly immersing students in professional environments. Through internships, apprenticeships, job shadowing, and co-op experiences, students get to apply what they've learned, see how industries operate, and explore career paths firsthand in a meaningful way. This combination is especially valuable in high-demand fields, such as construction, technology, healthcare, and the skilled trades—industries that rely on strong technical ability and practical experience. By engaging in CTE and participating in WBL opportunities, students gain confidence, develop essential workplace skills, build professional networks, and make more informed decisions about their futures. Together, CTE and WBL create a clear, supported pathway from school to employment, training, or college.

TYPES OF WORK-BASED LEARNING OPPORTUNITIES

Internships
A behind-the-scenes look at your future career. Internships let you spend weeks or months learning how a real workplace operates while gaining experience that looks great on a résumé.

Apprenticeships
An in-depth, paid learning experience that combines on-the-job training with classroom instruction. Apprentices earn while they learn and can graduate with industry-recognized credentials, certifications, and a direct pathway into a high-demand career.

Job Shadowing
A short-term, low-pressure way to explore careers by spending a day or two observing a professional on the job. Perfect for students who want to "try on" different career paths before committing.

Cooperative Education (Co-op)
A structured blend of school and work. You'll spend part of your week learning in the classroom and the other part applying those skills on the job. Co-ops help students connect academics with real-world work experience.

BENEFITS OF WORK-BASED LEARNING

Real-World Experience
See for yourself what different jobs are actually like—no guessing, no Googling. WBL helps you understand work expectations, industry culture, and day-to-day responsibilities.

Skill Development
Grow technical skills, communication skills, problem-solving abilities, and professional habits employers look for. These experiences help you stand out when applying for jobs or training programs.

Networking Opportunities
WBL introduces you to professionals, mentors, and future employers who can open doors, offer guidance, and help you find your next opportunity.

Increased Confidence
Working in real settings builds confidence in your abilities, helps you refine your goals, and prepares you for a smooth transition into employment, training, or college.

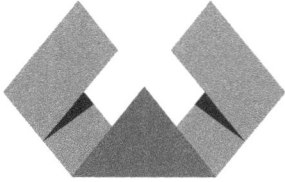

WORK-BASED LEARNING CONTINUUM

THE WHITE-LABEL MANAGEMENT WBL CONTINUUM TRANSFORMS CLASSROOM LEARNING INTO REAL OPPORTUNITIES BY GUIDING STUDENTS THROUGH CLEAR, CONNECTED PATHWAYS FROM EDUCATION TO EMPLOYMENT.

7th-8th GRADES

CAREER AWARENESS

Learn abut a wide variety of jobs and careers.

Structured Learning
- Virtual workplace tours
- Career exploration lessons
- Guest speakers
- Career aptitude and interest assessment

Work-Based Learning Elements
- Provide authentic and engaging experiences
- Create career exposure opportunities
- Provide orientations and support for students and their families

"I understand the opportunities available and am beginning to discover what I might want to peruse."

9th-10th GRADES

CAREER EXPLORATION

Explore career interests and plan for the future.

Structured Learning
- Career exploration lessons
- Career research
- Guest speakers
- Career aptitude and interest assessment

Work-Based Learning Elements
- Create career exposure opportunities
- Provide orientations and support for students and their families

"I'm interested in this field and am beginning to understand what it's about and what it takes to pursue a career."

11th GRADE

CAREER EXPLORATION

Explore career interests
and plan for the future.

Structured Learning
- Career and technical education
- Work readiness activities
- Career research
- Internships

Work-Based Learning Elements
- Individual career plans
- Exposure to authentic work-world experiences
- Provide orientations and support for students and their families

"I know the kinds of things I want to do, and I'm getting the chance to build new skills and practice applying them."

12th GRADE

CAREER EXPLORATION

Explore career interests
and plan for the future.

Structured Learning
- Career and technical education
- Work readiness activities
- Career coaching and planning
- Pre-apprenticeships

Work-Based Learning Elements
- Connect the experience with actionable next steps
- Exposure to authentic work-world experiences
- Provide orientations and support for students and their families

"I know the kinds of things I want to do, and I'm prepared to take advantage of the opportunities ahead."

POST GRADUATION

CAREER EXPLORATION

Explore career interests
and plan for the future.

Structured Learning
- Entry-level career connects
- Work readiness activities
- Career coaching and planning
- Pre-apprenticeships

Work-Based Learning Elements
- Connect the experience with actionable next steps
- Exposure to authentic work-world experiences
- Document progress

"I'm prepared to access employment opportunities."

CAREER PATHWAYS

ADVANCED MANUFACTURING & ENGINEERING

Explore
MY PATH

INDUSTRY OVERVIEW:

Did you know North Carolina used to be the cool kid on the block when it came to making stuff like tobacco, textiles, and furniture? Well, the state's seriously upped its game since then. Now it's rocking the advanced manufacturing scene, with the biggest workforce in the Southeast. That's pretty rad, right? The state's job market is on fire, too, with over 445,000 new gigs expected to pop up between 2021 and 2030. And get this—even though some old-school manufacturing is taking a hit, the industry as a whole is still going to grow by about 22,200 jobs. Not too shabby!

GROWTH PROJECTIONS:

So, what's the next big thing in North Carolina? Electric cars and lithium batteries, baby! In 2023, a bunch of companies making electric vehicles and battery parts were like, "Yeah, we're setting up shop here," and dropped nearly $10 billion in investments in the state. That's some serious cash! But wait, there's more. The state's also got a ton of aerospace stuff going on, from making parts to fixing planes. Oh, and don't forget about the eight military bases with airborne units and flight operations. It's like North Carolina's becoming the go-to spot for anything that moves, whether it's on the ground or in the air. Pretty cool, huh?

TYPES OF PRODUCTS AND SERVICES PRODUCED IN ADVANCED MANUFACTURING & ENGINEERING IN NORTH CAROLINA:

Aircraft components: Production of precision-engineered parts for aircraft, including turbine blades and aerospace fasteners, to support the aviation and defense industries.

Automotive parts: Manufacturing of high-performance vehicle components, such as engines, transmissions, and brake systems, for leading global automakers.

Pharmaceuticals: Advanced manufacturing of biopharmaceuticals and small-molecule drugs, leveraging cutting-edge technologies in precision medicine.

Medical devices: Development and production of diagnostic equipment, surgical tools, and wearable health monitors for healthcare providers.

Semiconductors: Fabrication of microchips and semiconductors critical for consumer electronics, industrial applications, and telecommunications.

Renewable energy equipment: Design and production of solar panels, wind turbine components, and battery storage systems to advance clean energy solutions.

ADVANCED MANUFACTURING & ENGINEERING COMPANIES IN NORTH CAROLINA:

1. **AGY:** A world leader in high-performance materials used in various markets, including electronics, thermoplastics, industrial, aerospace, recreation/consumer, and defense.

2. **Pfizer:** A global pharmaceutical company with a manufacturing facility in Rocky Mount, NC, working to apply science and global resources to bring therapies to people that extend and significantly improve their lives.

3. **Toyota:** A multinational automotive manufacturer that recently announced plans to establish a major battery manufacturing plant in Greensboro, NC.

4. **JELD-WEN:** A global manufacturer of interior and exterior building products, windows, and doors whose mission is to design, produce, and distribute an extensive range of interior and exterior doors; wood, vinyl, and aluminum windows; and related products.

5. **Baxter:** A global healthcare company with operations in North Carolina working to apply science and global resources to bring therapies to people that extend and significantly improve their lives.

6. **Biogen:** A multinational biotechnology company based in North Carolina whose mission is to discover, develop, and deliver innovative health solutions that advance the prevention and treatment of diseases in people and animals.

7. **Eli Lilly:** A global pharmaceutical company with operations in North Carolina working to discover, develop, manufacture, and market pharmaceutical products for humans and animals.

8. **Grifols:** A global healthcare company with a significant presence in North Carolina whose mission is to enhance the health and well-being of people worldwide.

9. **Merck & Co:** A multinational pharmaceutical company with operations in North Carolina that aims to discover, develop, manufacture, and market pharmaceutical products for humans and animals.

10. **Coca-Cola Consolidated:** The largest Coca-Cola bottler in the US, making, selling, and distributing beverages of The Coca-Cola Company and other partner companies, with bases in the US Southeast, Midwest, and Mid-Atlantic regions.

WORKPLACE COMPETENCIES:

1	Problem-Solving and Decision-Making	Identifying and analyzing problems in manufacturing processes and developing practical solutions.
2	Teamwork and Collaboration	Working effectively with colleagues, supervisors, and cross-functional teams to achieve common goals. Contributing to a positive team environment and being open to feedback and collaboration.
3	Communication	Clearly and effectively communicating information, ideas, and instructions to team members and management.
4	Time Management	Prioritizing tasks and efficiently managing time to meet production deadlines and targets. Balancing multiple responsibilities and maintaining productivity under pressure.
5	Adaptability and Flexibility	Being open to new ideas, learning opportunities, and changes in workplace practices.

PERSONAL COMPETENCIES:

1	Dependability and Responsibility	Taking ownership of work and being accountable for personal performance and results.
2	Initiative and Self-Motivation	Proactively seeking out tasks, responsibilities, and learning opportunities without being prompted. Demonstrating a strong work ethic and a desire to continuously improve and excel.
3	Continuous Learning	Actively pursuing new knowledge, skills, and competencies relevant to advanced manufacturing.
4	Stress Management and Resilience	Effectively managing stress and maintaining performance under pressure.
5	Professionalism	Displaying professional attitudes and behaviors, including punctuality, respect for others, and appropriate workplace conduct.

KEY KNOWLEDGE, SKILLS, AND ABILITIES:

Now we're getting to the good stuff! Here's a list of crucial knowledge, skills, and abilities essential for success in the manufacturing industry. They'll ensure that you are productive and safe in the workplace.

KNOWLEDGE	SKILLS	ABILITIES
Familiarity with workplace safety and health regulations to ensure compliance and maintain a safe working environment.	Careful monitoring and quality control to ensure that products meet specifications and standards.	Capability to evaluate complex situations and make decisions that ensure efficiency and quality in manufacturing.

RECOMMENDED HIGH SCHOOL COURSES TO PREPARE FOR A CAREER IN ADVANCED MANUFACTURING & ENGINEERING

1	Introduction to Manufacturing Technology	This course provides a foundational understanding of motion, energy, and forces, essential for understanding how machinery and manufacturing systems work.
2	Geometry and Trigonometry	A strong foundation in geometry and trigonometry is essential to understanding spatial relationships, measurements, and design principles. These skills are directly applicable to architecture and various engineering fields.
3	Physics	Physics provides an understanding of forces, energy, and motion—key concepts in both engineering and architecture. Building design and structural engineering concepts require a solid grasp of physical laws.
4	Introduction to Engineering or Pre-Engineering	These courses introduce students to the basic principles of engineering, problem-solving, and the engineering design process, providing them with a head start in understanding the industry's core concepts.
5	Computer-Aided Design (CAD)	This course teaches students how to use software to create technical drawings and 3D models, a crucial skill in product design and engineering.

TOP 10 OCCUPATIONS IN
ADVANCED MANUFACTURING & ENGINEERING:

Rank	Occupation	Education/Training	Average Wage
1	Welder	High school diploma or equivalent, along with technical and on-the-job training.	$43,000–$57,766 per year
2	Maintenance Technician	High school diploma or equivalent; technical training or an associate's degree may be preferred.	$37,500–$49,794 per year
3	Technical Support Specialist	Bachelor's degree in computer science or a related field.	$54,916 per year
4	Field Service Technician	High school diploma or equivalent; postsecondary nondegree award or associate's degree.	$57,088 per year
5	Manufacturing Technician	Associate's degree in engineering or manufacturing technology.	$60,201 per year
6	Quality Assurance Inspector	High school diploma or equivalent; on-the-job training or a certificate.	$52,788 per year
7	Industrial Engineering Technologist	Associate's degree or postsecondary certificate.	$62,610 per year
8	Manufacturing Engineer	Bachelor's degree in industrial engineering or a related field.	$71,169 per year
9	Production Supervisor	Bachelor's degree in business administration, industrial technology, or engineering.	$51,000–$71,169 per year
10	Plant Manager	Bachelor's or master's degree in business administration, industrial management, or engineering.	$53,000–$74,169 per year

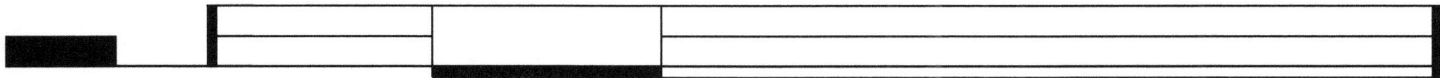

MY NOTES:

CAREER PATHWAYS

ANIMAL SCIENCE

Explore
MY PATH

INDUSTRY OVERVIEW:

Did you know that North Carolina is a superstar in farming and animal science? It's like combining farming with science class—in the coolest way possible! The state is huge in raising chickens, pigs, and cows (we're talking massive farms!), and it's got experts who are like nutritionists but for farm animals, making sure all the animals get the best food to stay healthy. There are also tons of animal doctors (vets) keeping these animals in good shape, plus smart scientists in labs working on making farming even better. If you were playing a video game where you had to build the perfect farm state, North Carolina would be getting a high score! There are big farms everywhere, along with colleges and research centers trying to figure out how to keep animals healthy and strong, make farms better for the environment, and make sure farming stays good for future generations. Animal science is pretty much the perfect mix of hands-on work and high-tech science!

GROWTH PROJECTIONS:

North Carolina's animal science industry is expected to see sustained growth as consumer demand for ethically produced and environmentally sustainable animal products increases. Biotechnology advancements, precision livestock farming, and improved veterinary care are driving growth, with an estimated annual increase of 5%–6%. This will create more opportunities for skilled workers in livestock management, animal health, genetics, and nutrition.

TYPES OF PRODUCTS AND SERVICES PRODUCED IN ANIMAL SCIENCE IN NORTH CAROLINA:

Poultry meat and eggs: North Carolina is a major producer of chicken and turkey meat and eggs, with large-scale operations throughout the state.

Beef cattle and dairy products: North Carolina has a substantial beef and dairy industry, producing various meat cuts and dairy products, such as milk and cheese.

Aquaculture: The state's aquaculture sector includes freshwater and marine species, producing fish and shellfish for food and ornamental purposes.

Animal feed formulation and production: North Carolina produces specialized animal feeds tailored to different livestock and poultry species, often utilizing locally grown crops.

Veterinary services and animal health products: The state offers comprehensive veterinary care and produces various animal health products, supporting both livestock and companion animals.

ANIMAL SCIENCE COMPANIES IN NORTH CAROLINA:

1. **Butterball, LLC:** A major American producer of turkey products, known for its whole turkeys and various processed turkey items.

2. **Prestage Farms:** A large family-owned pork and poultry producer based in North Carolina, known for its integrated farming operations.

3. **Smithfield Foods:** One of the world's largest pork processors and hog producers, with a significant presence in packaged meats.

4. **Nowymes:** A Danish biotechnology company specializing in enzyme and microbial technologies for various industries, including food and agriculture.

5. **Zoetis:** A global animal health company that develops, manufactures, and commercializes medicines, vaccines, and diagnostic products for pets and livestock.

6. **Merck Animal Health:** A division of Merck & Co focused on veterinary pharmaceuticals, vaccines, and health management solutions for animals.

7. **Mountaire Farms:** One of the largest chicken producers in the US, known for its vertically integrated poultry operations.

8. **Charles River Laboratories:** A global provider of laboratory services, including animal research models, for the pharmaceutical, biotechnology, and medical device industries.

9. **House-Autry Mills:** A North Carolina–based company known for producing breading, cornmeal, and other Southern-style food products.

10. **Elanco Animal Health:** A global animal health company that provides products and services to improve animal health and food animal production.

WORKPLACE COMPETENCIES:

1	Team Collaboration	Ability to work with farmers, veterinarians, nutritionists, and other stakeholders.
2	Technological Proficiency	Competence in using precision farming technologies, data analytics for livestock management, and veterinary diagnostics.
3	Regulatory Compliance	Knowledge of animal welfare standards and environmental regulations.
4	Problem-Solving and Decision-Making	Ability to identify and resolve issues related to animal health, feed, and production efficiency.

PERSONAL COMPETENCIES:

1	Ethical Standards	High integrity in maintaining animal welfare and food safety.
2	Adaptability	Flexibility in working with new technologies and evolving industry standards.
3	Continuous Learning	Pursuit of ongoing professional development in animal care, genetics, and biotechnology.
4	Resilience	Ability to manage the physical demands and emotional stress of working with animals.

KEY KNOWLEDGE, SKILLS, AND ABILITIES:

KNOWLEDGE	SKILLS	ABILITIES
Familiarity with animal physiology, genetics, nutrition, and disease control; ethical standards in animal production; veterinary care; and biotechnology.	Animal handling, laboratory research, data analysis, problem-solving, technical skills in animal care, and feed formulation.	Strong communication skills, ability to work with animals under varying conditions, and adaptability to new agricultural technologies.

RECOMMENDED HIGH SCHOOL COURSES TO PREPARE FOR A CAREER IN ANIMAL SCIENCE:

1	**Biology**	This course covers the fundamental principles of life science, including genetics, anatomy, and ecosystems, which are essential to understanding animal biology and health.
2	**Agricultural Science**	This course introduces students to the principles of farming, animal husbandry, and sustainable agriculture, providing a solid background in the core concepts of animal production.
3	**Chemistry**	Understanding chemical processes is crucial for careers in animal nutrition, veterinary medicine, and biotechnology. This course teaches students about the chemical reactions, compounds, and elements that play a role in animal science.
4	**Environmental Science**	This course focuses on the interactions between organisms and their environments, which are important in sustainable livestock farming, animal health, and ecosystem management.
5	**Anatomy and Physiology**	This course teaches students about the structure and function of animals, preparing them for roles in veterinary science, animal breeding, and animal research.

TOP 10 OCCUPATIONS IN ANIMAL SCIENCE:

Rank	Occupation	Education/Training	Average Wage
1	Animal Nutritionist	Bachelor's or master's degree in animal nutrition or animal science.	$70,000–$85,000 per year
2	Veterinarian	Doctor of Veterinary Medicine.	$90,000–$120,000 per year
3	Animal Breeder	Bachelor's degree in animal science or genetics.	$50,000–$65,000 per year
4	Livestock Manager	Bachelor's degree in animal science or agribusiness.	$60,000–$80,000 per year
5	Animal Geneticist	Master's or PhD in animal science or genetics.	$75,000–$95,000 per year
6	Veterinary Technician	Associates degree in veterinary technology.	$35,000–$45,000 per year
7	Meat Scientist	Bachelor's degree in animal science or food science.	$60,000–$80,000 per year
8	Animal Scientist	Master's or PhD in animal science.	$70,000–$100,000 per year
9	Farm Manager	Bachelor's degree in agriculture or animal science.	$55,000–$75,000 per year
10	Veterinary Pharmacologist	PhD in veterinary pharmacology or a related field.	$80,000–$110,000 per year

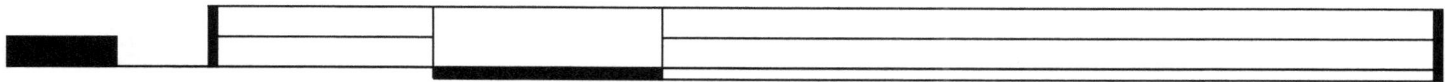

MY NOTES:

CAREER PATHWAYS

ARCHITECTURE & ENGINEERING

INDUSTRY OVERVIEW:

Ever wonder who's behind all those cool buildings and bridges popping up around North Carolina? It's the architecture and engineering (A&E) crew! These folks are the masterminds of our state's infrastructure. They're not just building stuff—they're shaping our cities, helping other industries grow, and even looking out for our planet. We're talking about everything from designing skyscrapers to figuring out how to make our energy cleaner. North Carolina's got some pretty awesome A&E firms that are always coming up with new ways to make our state even better.

GROWTH PROJECTIONS:

Here's the exciting part—this industry is on fire! We're looking at some serious growth in the next few years. Why? Well, North Carolina's putting big bucks into building new stuff, fixing up old things, and making everything more eco-friendly. We're talking about a 6%–8% boost every year for the next decade. That means more jobs for architects, engineers, and all sorts of cool cats in the construction world. So if you're into designing the future or building things that last, North Carolina's A&E scene just might be your jam!

TYPES OF PRODUCTS AND SERVICES PRODUCED IN ARCHITECTURE & ENGINEERING IN NORTH CAROLINA:

Structural engineering services: Expert design and analysis of the load-bearing elements of buildings and other infrastructure.

Civil engineering for urban development: Planning and design of roads, bridges, and public utilities to support growing cities.

Geotechnical engineering reports: Soil and rock analysis to ensure proper foundation design and site stability.

Green infrastructure design: Integration of natural systems into urban landscapes for stormwater management and environmental benefits.

Transportation engineering: Planning and design of efficient and safe transportation networks, including highways and public transit systems.

ARCHITECTURE & ENGINEERING COMPANIES IN NORTH CAROLINA:

1. **Kimley-Horn and Associates, Inc:** A premier planning and design consulting firm offering a wide range of services in civil engineering, transportation, and land planning across the US.

2. **Clark Nexsen:** An A&E firm known for its innovative and sustainable designs across various sectors, including education, government, and commercial projects.

3. **McAdams Company:** A multidisciplinary civil engineering and land planning firm specializing in site development, infrastructure design, and environmental services.

4. **Stewart Engineering, Inc:** A comprehensive engineering, design, and planning firm offering services in structural engineering, geomatics, and construction management.

5. **Little Diversified Architectural Consulting:** An international architecture and design firm that provides innovative solutions for various sectors, including healthcare, education, and commercial spaces.

6. **S&ME, Inc:** A geotechnical and environmental engineering firm offering services in materials testing, construction services, and natural resources management.

7. **Dewberry:** A nationwide professional services firm specializing in engineering, architecture, and consulting services for both public and private sector clients.

8. **Gensler:** A global architecture, design, and planning firm known for creating innovative and human-centered spaces across various industries and scales.

9. **STV Group, Inc:** A multidisciplinary engineering and architectural firm providing services in transportation, infrastructure, buildings, and construction management.

10. **HDR Engineering, Inc:** A global firm offering engineering, architecture, environmental, and construction services across various sectors, including water, transportation, and healthcare.

WORKPLACE COMPETENCIES:

1	Collaboration and Teamwork	Ability to work effectively with interdisciplinary teams (architects, engineers, and planners).
2	Technological Proficiency	Competence in using software like AutoCAD, building information modeling, and project management tools.
3	Project Management	Management of timelines, resources, and budgets to ensure project success.
4	Client Focus	Strong understanding of client needs and the ability to translate those into functional design and engineering solutions.
5	Safety Awareness	Knowledge of safety standards and compliance with regulatory requirements.

PERSONAL COMPETENCIES:

1	Attention to Detail	Precision in design, calculation, and project execution to avoid costly errors.
2	Adaptability	Ability to adjust to new technologies, client demands, and regulatory changes.
3	Problem-Solving and Decision-Making	Quick identification of solutions to unexpected challenges on projects.
4	Ethics and Integrity	Maintaining high professional standards and ensuring compliance with safety and environmental regulations.
5	Continuous Learning	Staying up-to-date with advancements in engineering, architecture, and construction technology.

KEY KNOWLEDGE, SKILLS, AND ABILITIES:

KNOWLEDGE	SKILLS	ABILITIES
Familiarity with building codes, materials science, environmental sustainability, civil engineering principles, and architectural design.	Proficiency with computer-aided design (CAD) software, project management, spatial awareness, communication, and analytical thinking.	Problem-solving, attention to detail, adaptability to new technologies, and the ability to work under pressure.

RECOMMENDED HIGH SCHOOL COURSES TO PREPARE FOR A CAREER IN ARCHITECTURE & ENGINEERING:

1	Geometry and Trigonometry	A strong foundation in geometry and trigonometry is essential to understand spatial relationships, measurements, and the principles of design.
2	Physics	Physics provides an understanding of forces, energy, and motion—key concepts in both engineering and architecture.
3	CAD or Drafting	Learning how to use CAD software is crucial for those entering A&E, as it is the standard technology used to create technical drawings and design plans.
4	Introduction to Engineering or Pre-Engineering	These courses introduce students to the basic principles of engineering, problem-solving, and the engineering design process, providing them with a head start in understanding the industry's core concepts.
5	Environmental Science	Understanding environmental impacts, sustainability practices, and energy-efficient design is becoming increasingly important.

TOP 10 OCCUPATIONS IN ARCHITECTURE & ENGINEERING:

Rank	Occupation	Education/Training	Average Wage
1	**Civil Engineer**	Bachelor's degree in civil engineering; professional engineer (PE) license.	$83,000 per year
2	**Architect**	Bachelor's or master's degree in architecture; architect license.	$82,000 per year
3	**Mechanical Engineer**	Bachelor's degree in mechanical engineering.	$85,000 per year
4	**Structural Engineer**	Bachelor's or master's degree in civil or structural engineering; PE license.	$87,000 per year
5	**Construction Manager**	Bachelor's degree in construction management, engineering, or architecture.	$89,000 per year
6	**Environmental Engineer**	Bachelor's degree in environmental engineering.	$82,000 per year
7	**Urban Planner**	Master's degree in urban planning or a related field.	$75,000 per year
8	**Electrical Engineer**	Bachelor's degree in electrical engineering.	$88,000 per year
9	**Landscape Architect**	Bachelor's or master's degree in landscape architecture; license required.	$70,000 per year
10	**Surveyor**	Bachelor's degree in surveying or geomatics; license required.	$65,000 per year

MY NOTES:

CAREER PATHWAYS

BIOMEDICAL SCIENCE

Explore
MY PATH

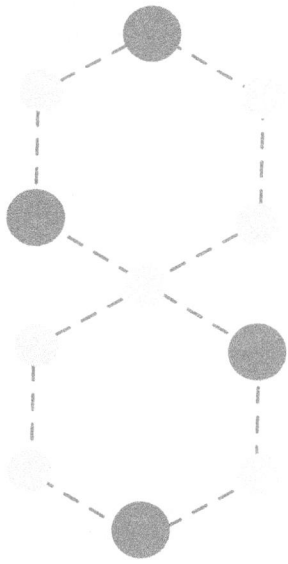

INDUSTRY OVERVIEW:

Did you know North Carolina is crushing it in the biomedical science game? This field is like the cool kid of the state's economy, specializing in some pretty sweet stuff like biotech, pharma, and life sciences. There's this place called Research Triangle Park that's basically a playground for science nerds—in a good way! It's packed with research institutions and companies doing all sorts of mind-blowing stuff with medical devices, new treatments, and clinical trials. And get this: They're pumping more money into making biopharmaceuticals and messing around with gene therapy. North Carolina's definitely not holding back when it comes to being a biomedical big shot.

GROWTH PROJECTIONS:

So, what's next for this biomedical hotspot? Buckle up, because it's looking pretty exciting! The industry's expected to grow like crazy, especially in biotech and pharmaceuticals. We're talking about a 6%–7% increase every year—that's no joke! And it's not just about the numbers. With all the cool new stuff happening in personalized medicine (yeah, medicine just for you!), gene therapy, and fancy new ways to make drugs, there's going to be a ton of job opportunities available. If you're into science and want a career that's basically future-proof, you might want to check out what's going down in North Carolina's biomedical scene.

TYPES OF PRODUCTS AND SERVICES PRODUCED IN BIOMEDICAL SCIENCE IN NORTH CAROLINA:

Pharmaceutical drugs: Medications developed and manufactured to treat various diseases and health conditions.

Medical devices: Instruments, apparatuses, or machines used for the diagnosis, treatment, or monitoring of medical conditions.

Bioinformatics software: Specialized computer programs designed to analyze and interpret biological data, particularly in genomics and proteomics.

Biomedical imaging equipment: Advanced imaging technologies used for medical diagnosis and research, such as MRI or CT scanners.

Vaccine development and production: Research, development, and manufacturing of vaccines to prevent infectious diseases.

BIOMEDICAL SCIENCE COMPANIES IN NORTH CAROLINA:

1. **Biogen:** A multinational biotechnology company specializing in the discovery, development, and delivery of therapies for neurological and neurodegenerative diseases.

2. **Labcorp:** A leading global life sciences company providing comprehensive clinical laboratory and end-to-end drug development services.

3. **Pfizer:** One of the world's largest pharmaceutical corporations, known for its wide range of medicines and vaccines, including the COVID-19 vaccine developed with BioNTech.

4. **IQVIA:** A multinational company serving the combined industries of health information technology (IT) and clinical research, providing advanced analytics, technology solutions, and contract research services.

5. **GRAIL, Inc:** A healthcare company focused on early cancer detection through innovative blood-based screening technologies.

6. **Precision BioSciences:** A genome editing company dedicated to improving life through the use of its ARCUS genome editing platform in therapeutic and food applications.

7. **BioCryst Pharmaceuticals:** A biotechnology company focused on the development of novel, oral small-molecule medicines that treat rare diseases.

8. **Novartis Gene Therapies:** A division of Novartis dedicated to developing and commercializing gene therapies for patients and families devastated by rare and life-threatening neurological genetic diseases.

9. **Advocate Health:** A company headquartered in Charlotte, NC—and working to advance health equity and improve access and affordability for the people and communities it serves.

10. **Novant Health:** A four-state integrated network of physician clinics, outpatient centers, and hospitals across the Southeast US.

WORKPLACE COMPETENCIES:

1	Teamwork and Collaboration	Working cohesively with interdisciplinary teams, including scientists, engineers, and healthcare professionals, to achieve shared goals in research and development.
2	Adaptability and Flexibility	Adjusting to rapidly changing technologies, protocols, and regulations in biomedical research and healthcare environments. This includes being open to new ideas and approaches.
3	Attention to Detail	Ensuring precision in all aspects of work, from experimental setups and data recording to regulatory compliance and patient safety protocols.
4	Communication Skills	Clearly articulating research findings, technical information, and project goals to diverse audiences, including colleagues, regulatory bodies, and the public.
5	Time Management and Organization	Prioritizing tasks effectively to meet deadlines in research, clinical trials, or manufacturing while maintaining high standards of quality and accuracy.

PERSONAL COMPETENCIES:

1	Dependability and Responsibility	Being reliable, punctual, and consistent in completing assigned tasks. Professionals in biomedical science often handle sensitive data and research where accuracy and accountability are crucial.
2	Continuous Learning	Demonstrating a commitment to staying updated with the latest advancements in biomedical research, technologies, and regulations. This includes attending workshops, obtaining certifications, and reading scientific literature.
3	Ethical Integrity	Upholding strong ethical standards, especially in research and clinical practices, to ensure patient safety, data integrity, and adherence to industry regulations.
4	Resilience and Stress Management	Effectively managing stress while working in high-pressure environments such as laboratories, clinical trials, or regulatory settings. This includes maintaining focus and composure during setbacks.
5	Critical Thinking and Problem-Solving	Analyzing complex situations, data, or research findings to develop innovative solutions and make informed decisions.

KEY KNOWLEDGE, SKILLS, AND ABILITIES:

KNOWLEDGE	SKILLS	ABILITIES
Familiarity with molecular biology, pharmacology, clinical trials, and regulatory guidelines.	Data analysis, laboratory techniques, project management, and bioinformatics software proficiency.	Critical thinking, problem-solving, attention to detail, and communication of complex scientific concepts.

RECOMMENDED HIGH SCHOOL COURSES TO PREPARE FOR A CAREER IN BIOMEDICAL SCIENCE:

1	**Biology**	This course provides a foundational understanding of living organisms, cells, and biological processes, which is essential for careers in biomedical science.
2	**Chemistry**	This course is critical to understanding chemical reactions, compounds, and processes, which are fundamental in biomedical science, particularly in pharmacology and biochemistry.
3	**Mathematics (Algebra, Geometry, and Calculus)**	Mathematical skills are crucial for data analysis, use of statistical methods, and problem-solving in biomedical research and clinical trials.
4	**Physics**	This course is essential to understand the physical principles underlying medical devices, biotechnology equipment, and laboratory technologies.
5	**Health Science or Anatomy and Physiology**	This course offers an introduction to the human body, medical terminology, and healthcare systems, helping students become familiar with the clinical and health-related aspects of biomedical science.

TOP 10 OCCUPATIONS IN BIOMEDICAL SCIENCE:

Rank	Occupation	Education/Training	Average Wage
1	Biomedical Scientist	Bachelor's or master's degree in biomedical science or a related field.	$82,000 per year
2	Clinical Research Associate	Bachelor's degree in life or health sciences; certifications in clinical research.	$65,000 per year
3	Biostatistician	Master's degree in biostatistics, statistics, or epidemiology.	$90,000 per year
4	Medical Laboratory Technician	Associate's degree in clinical laboratory science; certification required.	$55,000 per year
5	Pharmaceutical Sales Representative	Bachelor's degree in life sciences or business.	$70,000 per year + commission
6	Regulatory Affairs Specialist	Bachelor's degree in life sciences; Regulatory Affairs Professionals Society certification.	$85,000 per year
7	Genetic Counselor	Master's degree in genetic counseling; board certification.	$81,000 per year
8	Bioprocess Engineer	Bachelor's or master's degree in chemical engineering or biotechnology.	$92,000 per year
9	Quality Control Analyst	Bachelor's degree in chemistry, biology, or biotechnology.	$60,000 per year
10	Medical Device Engineer	Bachelor's or master's degree in biomedical or mechanical engineering.	$94,000 per year

MY NOTES:

CAREER PATHWAYS

BUSINESS MANAGEMENT

Explore
MY PATH

INDUSTRY OVERVIEW:

Business management in North Carolina is all about steering the ship across various industries like finance, tech, and healthcare. It's not just pushing papers—these pros are the go-to people for making operations smoother, keeping teams motivated, and cooking up smart strategies to push businesses forward. The state's business-friendly vibe is attracting everyone from scrappy startups to big-league corporations, which means there's a growing need for savvy managers who can handle it all.

GROWTH PROJECTIONS:

Looking ahead, the future's bright for business management in North Carolina The state's experts predict a solid 7%–9% growth in this field over the next decade Why? As companies aim to expand, adapt to market curveballs, and step up their game, they need sharp leaders to guide the way So, if you're into calling the shots and making things happen, business management could be your ticket to an exciting career. The demand for skilled managers is on the rise, making this a field worth watching.

TYPES OF PRODUCTS AND SERVICES PRODUCED IN BUSINESS MANAGEMENT IN NORTH CAROLINA:

Management consulting services: Expert advice and guidance to help organizations improve their performance and efficiency.

Project management software: Digital tools designed to assist in planning, organizing, and tracking business projects from start to finish.

Business analytics and reporting tools: Data-driven solutions that help companies make informed decisions based on key performance indicators and trends.

Change management consulting: Specialized services to guide organizations through periods of significant transformation or restructuring.

Risk management services: Strategies and tools designed to identify, assess, and mitigate potential business risks and threats.

BUSINESS MANAGEMENT COMPANIES IN NORTH CAROLINA:

1. **Bank of America:** A multinational investment bank and financial services company headquartered in Charlotte, NC.

2. **Duke Energy:** One of the largest electric power holding companies in the US, providing electricity to millions of customers in the Southeast and Midwest.

3. **Honeywell:** A global conglomerate that produces a variety of commercial and consumer products, engineering services, and aerospace systems.

4. **Truist Financial Corporation:** A bank holding company formed by the merger of BB&T and SunTrust Banks, offering a wide range of financial services.

5. **Nucor Corporation:** The largest steel producer in the US, known for its use of electric arc furnaces and recycled steel in its manufacturing process.

6. **Labcorp:** A leading global life sciences company that provides vital information to help doctors, hospitals, pharmaceutical companies, researchers, and patients make clear and confident decisions.

7. **Advance Auto Parts:** A leading automotive aftermarket parts provider that serves both professional installers and do-it-yourself customers.

8. **Lowe's Companies, Inc:** The second-largest hardware chain in the US, offering home improvement and appliance products to homeowners, renters, and business customers.

9. **Compass Group USA:** A subsidiary of the world's largest contract food service company, providing food and support services to various sectors, including healthcare, education, and business.

10. **Red Ventures:** A portfolio of digital companies that brings consumers and brands together through customized online experiences across various industries.

WORKPLACE COMPETENCIES:

1	Collaboration	Ability to work effectively in teams and cross-functional groups.
2	Critical Thinking	Ability to assess situations and make data-driven decisions.
3	Technology Proficiency	Competence in using business software and tools.
4	Client Focus	Maintaining a strong focus on customer satisfaction.
5	Time Management	Prioritizing tasks and efficiently managing multiple projects.

PERSONAL COMPETENCIES:

1	Integrity	Demonstrating ethical behavior and honesty in all business dealings.
2	Adaptability	Ability to adjust to changing market conditions and business needs.
3	Initiative	Taking proactive steps to achieve business goals.
4	Resilience	Handling challenges and setbacks with composure.
5	Continuous Learning	Staying updated on business trends, technology, and leadership practices.

KEY KNOWLEDGE, SKILLS, AND ABILITIES:

KNOWLEDGE	SKILLS	ABILITIES
Ability to analyze business trends and develop strategies.	Clear, effective communication with stakeholders.	Proficiency in budgeting, financial planning, and forecasting.

RECOMMENDED HIGH SCHOOL COURSES TO PREPARE FOR A CAREER IN BUSINESS MANAGEMENT:

1	Business Studies	This course introduces basic business concepts, including management, marketing, and finance.
2	Accounting and Finance	This course provides foundational knowledge in financial literacy, accounting practices, and budget management.
3	Economics	This course helps students understand the principles of micro- and macroeconomics, which are essential in business decision-making.
4	Information Technology	This course familiarizes students with business software and data management tools, which are vital in today's tech-driven business world.
5	Leadership and Communication	This course helps students develop leadership skills, effective communication, and team collaboration techniques.

TOP 10 OCCUPATIONS IN BUSINESS MANAGEMENT:

Rank	Occupation	Education/Training	Average Wage
1	General Manager	Bachelor's degree in business or a related field; Master of Business Administration (MBA) preferred.	$128,000 per year
2	Operations Manager	Bachelor's degree in business or a related field.	$98,000 per year
3	Financial Manager	Bachelor's degree in finance or accounting; MBA.	$132,000 per year
4	Human Resources Manager	Bachelor's degree in human resources or business.	$110,000 per year
5	Marketing Manager	Bachelor's degree in marketing or business administration.	$105,000 per year
6	Project Manager	Bachelor's degree in business or engineering; Project Management Professional certification preferred.	$92,000 per year
7	Business Analyst	Bachelor's degree in business or finance.	$85,000 per year
8	IT Manager	Bachelor's degree in information systems or business.	$125,000 per year
9	Sales Manager	Bachelor's degree in business or a related field.	$118,000 per year
10	Supply Chain Manager	Bachelor's degree in supply chain management or business.	$99,000 per year

MY NOTES:

CAREER PATHWAYS

CONSTRUCTION

Explore
MY PATH

INDUSTRY OVERVIEW:

Construction is the industry that turns ideas, drawings, and "What if we built this?" conversations into the real-world structures, homes, schools, hospitals, bridges, stadiums, solar farms, and workplaces that keep North Carolina moving. As one of the state's largest and fastest-growing sectors, it relies on skilled craftsmen and craftswomen across dozens of trades to bring these projects to life. Construction professionals shape the places where people live, learn, work, and gather, whether they're pouring concrete, framing buildings, wiring complex electrical systems, welding steel, or installing HVAC equipment that keeps spaces safe and comfortable. The industry spans residential, commercial, industrial, and utility projects, along with transportation infrastructure and rapidly expanding green construction, such as EV charging stations and high-efficiency buildings. Simply put, if it stands tall, shelters people, or contains walls, wiring, or concrete, the construction industry built it, and this vital industry continues to build North Carolina's future.

GROWTH PROJECTIONS:

North Carolina's construction sector is booming, so much so that "Grab your hard hat, we've got work for the next 20 years," feels entirely accurate. According to the North Carolina Department of Commerce, the state's construction industry is projected to grow 8.16% by 2032, adding more than 20,000 new jobs over the next decade. Population growth, business expansion, and major investments in housing, commercial development, and energy infrastructure continue to drive strong demand across nearly every construction trade. Thousands of openings emerge each year in carpentry, electrical, HVAC, plumbing, concrete finishing, heavy equipment operation, and welding, with even more opportunities created as veteran workers retire. For emerging talent, this means strong wages, steady employment, and clear advancement pathways. Anyone willing to learn a craft and build their skills can confidently step into a high-demand, future-ready construction career.

TYPES OF PRODUCTS AND SERVICES PRODUCED IN CONSTRUCTION IN NORTH CAROLINA:

Residential Construction: Build and renovate homes, apartments, and housing developments. Carpenters, electricians, plumbers, masons, and HVAC techs are the stars here.

Commercial & Industrial Construction: Hospitals, theaters, corporate HQs, factories, and distribution centers demand multi-trade teams and advanced project management.

Utility & Energy Infrastructure: Water systems, power lines, solar fields, renewable energy structures, and EV charging stations. Electricians, line workers, and equipment operators are critical.

Transportation Infrastructure: Roads, bridges, airports, rail, and walkways—important, but only one sector within the broader construction landscape.

CONSTRUCTION COMPANIES IN NORTH CAROLINA:

1. **Barnhill Contracting Company:** A leading North Carolina builder specializing in highway construction, site development, and asphalt paving, known for delivering large-scale infrastructure projects across the state.

2. **Crowder Construction Company:** A family-owned contractor providing heavy civil, environmental, and industrial construction services, with expertise in water/wastewater facilities, energy projects, and transportation structures.

3. **ST Wooten Corporation:** A major construction firm focused on asphalt production, paving, heavy highway work, and bridge construction, supporting transportation and civil infrastructure projects statewide.

4. **FlatironDragados:** A national heavy civil contractor recognized for complex bridge, highway, and design-build projects, including major transportation and infrastructure improvements in the Carolinas.

5. **Turner Construction (Commercial):** A global commercial builder delivering high-performance office buildings, hospitals, stadiums, and corporate facilities with an emphasis on innovation, safety, and sustainable construction practices.

6. **Choate Construction:** A prominent commercial construction firm specializing in office, healthcare, institutional, and industrial projects, known for quality craftsmanship and collaborative project delivery.

7. **Rodgers Builders (Healthcare and Commercial):** A leading Southeast contractor with deep expertise in healthcare, higher education, and commercial construction, delivering complex projects in occupied and high-performance environments.

8. **Messer Construction:** A commercial builder focused on large-scale institutional projects, including healthcare, aviation, life sciences, and higher education facilities across the Southeast and Midwest.

9. **Blythe Construction:** One of the Carolinas' largest heavy civil contractors, specializing in asphalt paving, roadway construction, site work, and major transportation infrastructure projects.

10. **Zachry Construction Corporation:** A national heavy civil contractor specializing in complex infrastructure projects, including highways, bridges, transportation systems, and large-scale civil works, recognized for delivering high-quality, safety-driven construction across the country.

WORKPLACE COMPETENCIES:

1	Teamwork	Coordinating with colleagues in other trades; carpenters can't frame walls on top of electricians (again).
2	Problem-Solving	Fixing issues before the inspector arrives with a clipboard.
3	Time Management	Meeting deadlines in spite of harsh weather conditions, tight schedules, and material delivery issues.
4	Adaptability	Using new tools, tech, and green building methods.

PERSONAL COMPETENCIES:

1	Reliability	Showing up ready, on time, with PPE and maybe coffee.
2	Work Ethic	Staying focused through long days or tough conditions.
3	Resilience	Adapting to surprises, because job sites always have surprises.
4	Continuous Learning	Advancing through specialty certifications.

KEY KNOWLEDGE, SKILLS, AND ABILITIES:

KNOWLEDGE	SKILLS	ABILITIES
Understanding of construction materials, tools, and methods across multiple trades, including blueprint reading, construction math, and structural fundamentals. Familiarity with OSHA regulations, jobsite safety protocols, and applicable building and electrical codes.	Hands-on proficiency across core construction trades such as carpentry, concrete, electrical, welding, masonry, and interior finishing. Skilled in operating heavy equipment, using digital surveying and measurement tools, and applying technical knowledge to execute projects efficiently and accurately.	Strong problem-solving and adaptability in fast-paced, dynamic job-site environments. Demonstrated physical stamina, attention to detail, and the ability to work safely and collaboratively with multi-trade crews while communicating clearly with supervisors, inspectors, and team members.

RECOMMENDED HIGH SCHOOL COURSES TO PREPARE FOR A CAREER IN CONSTRUCTION:

1	**Construction Technology**	This course introduces students to basic building skills, tools, materials, and safety practices, providing hands-on experience that mirrors real construction job sites.
2	**Drafting and Design**	This class teaches students how to read and create technical drawings, blueprints, and digital models, which are essential for understanding how buildings and structures are planned.
3	**Geometry and Algebra**	These courses build the math skills used every day in construction, including measuring distances, calculating angles, estimating materials, and ensuring accurate layouts and dimensions.
4	**Physics**	This class helps students understand forces, motion, load, energy, and structural stability, which are fundamental concepts behind how buildings stand and why materials behave the way they do.
5	**CTE Pathways (Carpentry, HVAC, Electrical, Masonry, Engineering)**	These courses provide hands-on training and introductory certifications in skilled trades, giving students direct exposure to real construction careers and preparing them for apprenticeships or further technical training.

TOP 10 OCCUPATIONS IN CONSTRUCTION:

Rank	Occupation	Education/Training	Average Wage
1	Carpenter	Carpentry training program or apprenticeship.	$38,000–$55,000 per year
2	Electrician	State-approved electrical apprenticeship + licensure.	$45,000–$65,000 per year
3	Plumber/Pipefitter	Plumbing or pipefitting apprenticeship + state license.	$44,000–$62,000 per year
4	Heavy Equipment Operator	Heavy equipment operator training or certification.	$40,000–$58,000 per year
5	Construction Laborer	On-the-job training.	$34,000–$48,000 per year
6	Cement Mason/Concrete Finisher	Concrete finishing apprenticeship or trade training.	$40,000–$55,000 per year
7	HVAC Technician	HVAC training program + state licensure.	$45,000–$60,000 per year
8	Welder/Ironworker	Welding or ironworking technical training + certification.	$45,000–$65,000 per year
9	Project Manager	Bachelor's degree + project management certification.	$60,000–$95,000 per year
10	Civil Engineer	Bachelor's degree + professional engineer (PE) license.	$70,000–$100,000 per year

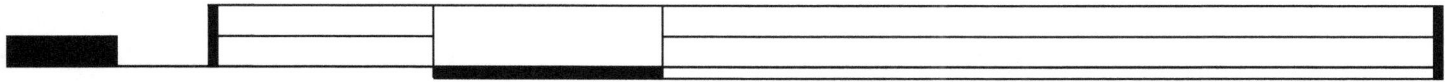

MY NOTES:

SECTION 7

CAREER PATHWAYS

COSMETOLOGY

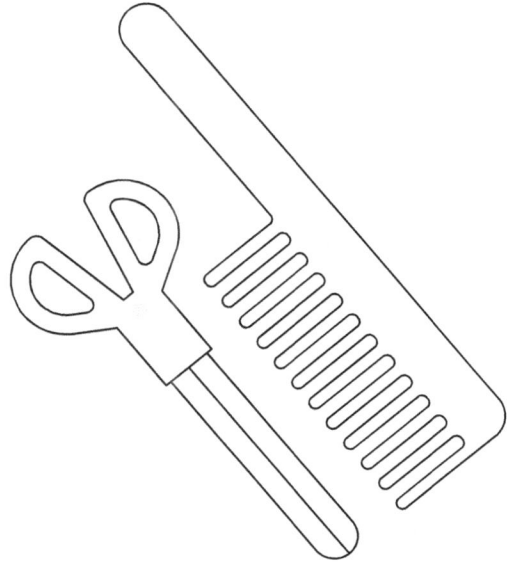

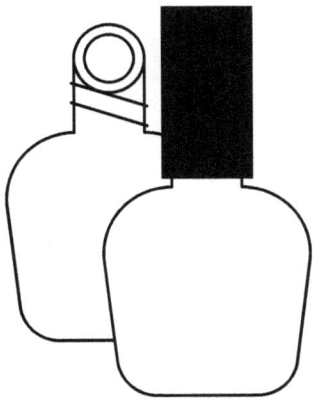

INDUSTRY OVERVIEW:

Hey there, beauty enthusiasts! Let's talk about the cosmetology scene in North Carolina. We're talking the whole package—hair, skin, nails, and makeup. People are getting more and more into looking their best, so this industry is making waves in the state's economy. North Carolina is packed with cool barbershops, salons, spas, and even companies whipping up awesome beauty products. And get this: There's a growing demand for beauty pros who can give people that personalized touch. We're seeing some cool trends, too, like eco-friendly beauty (save the planet while looking fab!) and high-tech skin treatments (hello, glow-up!).

GROWTH PROJECTIONS:

Let's peek into the future. The North Carolina cosmetology biz is set to blow up over the next 10 years, with an expected growth of 8%–10%. Why? Well, people are all about wellness and self-care these days, and let's be real—social media has us all wanting to look Instagram-ready 24/7. But here's the cool part: There's a rising demand for specialized services, like organic beauty products (because who doesn't want to look good naturally?) and natural hair care (curly girls, rejoice!). So, if you're thinking about jumping into this field, now's your chance to ride the wave and make your mark in the world of beauty!

TYPES OF PRODUCTS AND SERVICES PRODUCED IN COSMETOLOGY IN NORTH CAROLINA:

Nail care services: Manicures, pedicures, and nail enhancements performed by licensed technicians.

Natural hair care products: Organic and locally sourced hair care items tailored for various hair textures and types.

Makeup application services: Professional makeup artistry for special events, photoshoots, or everyday wear.

Eyelash extensions: Application of synthetic lashes to enhance the length and fullness of natural eyelashes.

Haircutting and styling services: Professional haircuts and styling techniques performed by licensed cosmetologists.

COSMETOLOGY COMPANIES IN NORTH CAROLINA:

1. **Ulta Beauty Salon:** A full-service beauty retailer and salon providing a wide range of cosmetics, skincare products, and hair services.

2. **No Grease Barbershop:** A modern barbershop chain that combines traditional grooming services with contemporary style and culture.

3. **Sport Clips:** A sports-themed hair salon franchise specializing in haircuts for men and boys in a casual, guy-friendly environment.

4. **Drybar:** A specialized salon chain focusing exclusively on blow-drying and styling services, without offering cuts or color.

5. **Massage Envy Spa & Salon:** A membership-based franchise offering professional massage therapy and skincare services in a spa-like setting.

6. **Phenix Salon Suites:** A company that offers rental suites for independent beauty professionals to operate their own businesses within a larger salon complex.

7. **Van Michael Salon:** An upscale hair salon known for its cutting-edge styles and high-end services, often associated with fashion and celebrity clientele.

8. **Great Clips:** A large, budget-friendly hair salon franchise offering quick and convenient haircuts for men, women, and children.

9. **Hand & Stone Massage and Facial Spa:** A franchise offering affordable massage therapy and facial services in a spa-like environment.

10. **The Duck's Feet Preen & Co:** A modern barbershop chain that combines traditional grooming services with contemporary style and culture.

WORKPLACE COMPETENCIES:

1	**Customer Service**	Ability to work within a crew on construction projects.
2	**Safety Awareness**	Strict adherence to industry regulations and best safety practices.
3	**Adaptability**	Flexibility to meet evolving construction needs and unexpected challenges.
4	**Technical Proficiency**	Familiarity with construction tools, equipment, and technologies.
5	**Retail and Business Acumen**	Effective task management to meet deadlines and budget constraints.

PERSONAL COMPETENCIES:

1	**Professionalism**	Maintaining a clean and welcoming environment.
2	**Creativity**	Innovating with styles and services.
3	**Empathy**	Listening to client needs and delivering personalized services.
4	**Attention to Detail**	Providing precision in beauty treatments to ensure customer satisfaction.

KEY KNOWLEDGE, SKILLS, AND ABILITIES:

KNOWLEDGE	SKILLS	ABILITIES
Strong understanding of hair care, skincare, nail care, and makeup techniques, including the science behind chemical treatments and anatomy.	Technical expertise in styling, cutting, and performing intricate beauty treatments; excellent customer service; time management; creativity; and the ability to sell beauty products.	Manual dexterity, strong color perception, physical stamina, problem-solving skills, and attention to detail.

RECOMMENDED HIGH SCHOOL COURSES TO PREPARE FOR A CAREER IN COSMETOLOGY:

1	**Anatomy and Physiology**	This course teaches human anatomy; knowledge of skin and hair structures is critical in providing beauty services.
2	**Chemistry**	This course is essential for understanding the chemical processes involved in hair coloring, skin treatments, and cosmetics.
3	**Art and Design**	This course encourages creativity and helps with the visual aspects of styling and makeup artistry.
4	**Business Management**	This course teaches the basics of running a salon or beauty-related business.
5	**Health Science**	This course provides knowledge on hygiene, safety, and personal care, which are vital in the beauty industry.

TOP 10 OCCUPATIONS IN COSMETOLOGY:

Rank	Occupation	Education/Training	Average Wage
1	Hair Stylist	Completion of a state-approved cosmetology program.	$25,000–$40,000 per year
2	Nail Technician	Completion of a state-approved nail technician program.	$22,000–$35,000 per year
3	Esthetician	Completion of a state-approved esthetician program.	$30,000–$45,000 per year
4	Barber	Completion of a state-approved barbering program.	$30,000–$45,000 per year
5	Makeup Artist	Certification from a makeup artistry school or cosmetology program; some states require licensure for makeup artists.	$35,000–$50,000 per year
6	Salon Manager	Cosmetology or related experience; business management course completion or salon management certification is often beneficial.	$40,000–$60,000 per year
7	Cosmetology Instructor	Cosmetology license; additional instructor certification; in North Carolina, several years of professional experience and state license.	$40,000–$55,000 per year
8	Waxing Specialist	Completion of a state-approved esthetician or cosmetology program with specialized training in waxing techniques; waxing license.	$28,000–$42,000 per year
9	Massage Therapist	Completion of a state-approved massage therapy program.	$35,000–$55,000 per year
10	Hair Color Specialist	Cosmetology program completion with advanced coursework or certification in hair coloring techniques; cosmetology license.	$32,000–$50,000 per year

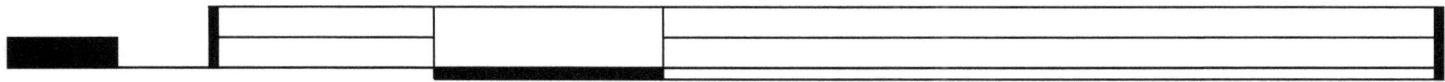

MY NOTES:

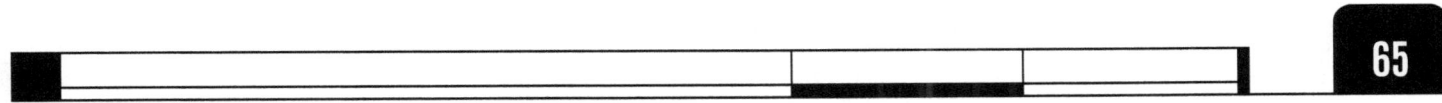

CAREER PATHWAYS

CULINARY ARTS & HOSPITALITY

Explore
MY PATH

INDUSTRY OVERVIEW:

Picture this: You're preparing to relocate to Charlotte, Raleigh, or Asheville. These cities are like food paradises, with killer restaurants and swanky hotels popping up left and right. And get this—schools like Central Piedmont Community College and Johnson & Wales University are churning out some seriously talented folks who are shaking things up in the industry. But wait, there's more! North Carolina's got beaches and mountains that tourists can't get enough of. That means plenty of opportunities to show off your culinary skills or hospitality magic. Plus, everyone's going crazy for sustainable eating, so if you're into that, you'll fit right in.

GROWTH PROJECTIONS:

Now, let's talk numbers. The big shots at the North Carolina Department of Commerce say this industry is going to grow by about 8% over the next 10 years. That's pretty sweet! With more people moving in and tourists flocking to our state, there's going to be a ton of demand for awesome dining experiences and top-notch hospitality.

And here's the really cool part: The state is becoming a hotspot for food innovation. We're talking mind-blowing food trucks, craft breweries, and restaurants. So, whether you want to be the next Top Chef or run a hotel that'll make the Ritz-Carlton jealous, North Carolina's got your back.

TYPES OF PRODUCTS AND SERVICES PRODUCED IN CULINARY ARTS & HOSPITALITY IN NORTH CAROLINA:

Craft breweries: Microbreweries producing unique, locally inspired beers that showcase the state's brewing heritage and innovative spirit.

Barbecue joints: Eateries specializing in North Carolina's distinct barbecue styles, including eastern and western variations of slow-cooked pork.

Seafood markets: Fresh seafood retailers providing locally caught fish and shellfish from North Carolina's extensive coastline.

Culinary tours: Guided experiences that take visitors through the state's food scene, exploring local specialties and hidden gems.

Food trucks: Mobile eateries offering diverse, innovative cuisine at events, festivals, and urban centers throughout the state.

CULINARY ARTS & HOSPITALITY COMPANIES IN NORTH CAROLINA:

1. **Compass Group USA:** A leading food and support services company operating in diverse sectors, including healthcare, education, and corporate dining.

2. **Sodexo:** A multinational corporation providing food services and facilities management to various industries worldwide.

3. **The Umstead Hotel and Spa:** A luxury five-star hotel and spa located in Cary, NC, known for its high-end accommodations and fine dining.

4. **Biltmore Estate:** A historic house museum and tourist attraction in Asheville, NC, featuring America's largest private residence and expansive gardens.

5. **Chef & the Farmer:** A farm-to-table restaurant in Kinston, NC, co-owned by Chef Vivian Howard and known for reimagining Southern cuisine.

6. **Vivace:** An upscale Italian restaurant with locations in Charlotte and Raleigh, NC, offering contemporary Italian cuisine in a stylish setting.

7. **Savor the Flavor Catering:** A North Carolina–based catering company providing customized menus and services for various events and occasions.

8. **McConnell Golf:** A golf club management company owning and operating multiple private golf clubs across the Carolinas and Tennessee.

9. **Krispy Kreme:** A global doughnut company and coffeehouse chain founded in Winston-Salem, NC, famous for its glazed doughnuts.

10. **The Fearrington House Restaurant:** An award-winning fine dining restaurant located in the Fearrington Village near Chapel Hill, NC, known for its farm-to-fork cuisine and extensive wine selection.

WORKPLACE COMPETENCIES:

1	Team Collaboration and Communication	Ability to work seamlessly with diverse teams in high-pressure environments and communicate effectively with coworkers and management.
2	Customer Service Excellence	Delivering exceptional guest experiences through attentiveness, problem-solving, and maintaining a positive demeanor.
3	Attention to Detail	Ensuring precision in food preparation, cleanliness, safety compliance, and overall service quality.
4	Time Management and Multitasking	Efficiently managing time to handle multiple responsibilities, such as food preparation, guest requests, and event setups, without compromising quality.
5	Technology and Equipment Proficiency	Using industry-specific tools and software, such as point-of-sale systems, reservation platforms, and kitchen equipment.

PERSONAL COMPETENCIES:

1	Adaptability and Resilience	Thriving in dynamic, high-stress environments and quickly adjusting to changing customer demands, staffing issues, or unexpected challenges.
2	Creativity and Innovation	Generating new ideas for menu items, event themes, or customer engagement strategies.
3	Ethical Decision-Making	Upholding integrity and fairness in handling customer interactions, team dynamics, and business practices.
4	Stress Management and Emotional Intelligence	Staying calm under pressure, managing stress effectively, and understanding others' emotions to foster a positive workplace environment.
5	Continuous Learning and Professional Growth	Commitment to lifelong learning through industry certifications, workshops, or staying updated on trends.

KEY KNOWLEDGE, SKILLS, AND ABILITIES:

KNOWLEDGE	SKILLS	ABILITIES
Familiarity with food safety standards, hospitality operations, customer service principles, culinary techniques, and beverage service.	Communication, culinary creativity, multitasking, customer interaction, and leadership.	Problem-solving, teamwork, management of multiple tasks, maintaining high service standards, and adaptability to customer preferences.

RECOMMENDED HIGH SCHOOL COURSES TO PREPARE FOR A CAREER IN CULINARY ARTS & HOSPITALITY:

1	**Culinary Arts I & II**	This course introduces students to basic cooking techniques, kitchen safety, food preparation, and recipe development. Advanced courses may cover menu planning, food presentation, and specialty cooking methods.
2	**Nutrition and Wellness**	This course focuses on understanding nutrition, healthy eating habits, and the impact of food choices on well-being. Students learn about meal planning, dietary guidelines, and food science.
3	**Hospitality and Tourism Management**	These courses cover the basics of hospitality operations, customer service, and the tourism industry. Students learn about event planning, hotel management, and restaurant operations.
4	**Business and Marketing**	This course teaches business management principles, marketing strategies, and entrepreneurship. Students gain knowledge about financial management, customer relations, and marketing campaigns.
5	**Food Science**	This course explores the scientific principles behind food production, processing, and safety. Topics include food chemistry, microbiology, and preservation methods.

TOP 10 OCCUPATIONS IN CULINARY ARTS & HOSPITALITY:

Rank	Occupation	Education/Training	Average Wage
1	Executive Chef	Culinary degree; extensive experience in leadership and kitchen management.	$63,000 per year
2	Sous Chef	Culinary degree; significant experience in professional kitchens.	$48,000 per year
3	Restaurant Manager	Bachelor's degree in hospitality management or equivalent experience.	$55,000 per year
4	Event Planner	Bachelor's degree in event or hospitality management; strong organizational skills.	$52,000 per year
5	Pastry Chef	Specialized pastry arts training.	$42,000 per year
6	Food and Beverage Director	Bachelor's degree in hospitality or business management; experience in strategic planning.	$80,000 per year
7	Catering Manager	Bachelor's degree in hospitality management or relevant work experience.	$50,000 per year
8	Hotel General Manager	Bachelor's degree in hospitality or business management.	$75,000 per year
9	Line Cook	Culinary training or apprenticeship.	$30,000 per year
10	Bar Manager	Experience in beverage management; certification in responsible alcohol service.	$45,000 per year

MY NOTES:

CAREER PATHWAYS

CUSTOMER RELATIONSHIP MANAGEMENT

Explore
MY PATH

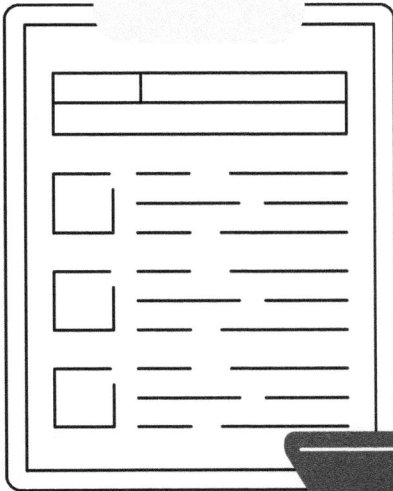

INDUSTRY OVERVIEW:

Hey there! Let's talk about customer relationship management (CRM) in North Carolina. It's basically all about helping businesses keep their customers happy and coming back for more. Think of it as the ultimate wingman for companies trying to build solid relationships with their clients. CRM is blowing up in North Carolina, especially in tech-savvy spots like Raleigh-Durham, Charlotte, and the Triad. Why? Well, all sorts of businesses—from tech startups to big healthcare companies—are realizing they need smart ways to manage their customer interactions. And CRM isn't just about boring old databases anymore. We're talking cloud stuff, artificial intelligence (AI), and some seriously cool data-crunching tools.

GROWTH PROJECTIONS:

Now, here's the exciting part—according to the state's Department of Commerce, CRM in North Carolina is set to grow like crazy. We're talking 10%–12% annually for the next 10 years! That's faster than you can say "customer satisfaction." This growth is coming from a few places. First, a ton of AI is being built into CRM systems, making them smarter than ever. Then, there's this big push for businesses to create awesome experiences for their customers. And let's not forget all those online shops popping up. They need CRM to keep track of who's buying what. So, if you're into tech and helping businesses crush it, CRM might just be your thing!

TYPES OF PRODUCTS AND SERVICES PRODUCED IN CUSTOMER RELATIONSHIP MANAGEMENT IN NORTH CAROLINA:

Cloud-based CRM software: Scalable, web-accessible platforms that allow businesses to manage customer interactions and data from anywhere.

Mobile CRM applications: Smartphone and tablet apps that enable sales teams to access and update customer information on the go.

CRM data analytics tools: Software that analyzes customer data to provide insights and predict future trends and behaviors.

Social media CRM platforms: Tools that monitor and manage customer interactions across various social media channels.

CRM training and education services: Programs and workshops that teach businesses how to effectively implement and use CRM systems.

CUSTOMER RELATIONSHIP MANAGEMENT COMPANIES IN NORTH CAROLINA:

1. **Red Hat (IBM):** A leading provider of open-source enterprise software solutions, now a subsidiary of IBM.

2. **Salesforce:** A cloud-based CRM platform offering a suite of applications for sales, services, marketing, and analytics.

3. **ChannelAdvisor:** An e-commerce software company that helps brands and retailers optimize their online sales across multiple marketplaces and digital marketing channels.

4. **PrecisionLender:** A software company specializing in pricing and profitability management solutions for commercial banks.

5. **Pendo:** A product experience platform that helps software companies improve their digital products through user analytics, feedback, and in-app guidance.

6. **Inmar Intelligence:** A technology-driven company providing data-driven solutions for retailers, manufacturers, healthcare providers, and government agencies.

7. **Bronto Software (Oracle NetSuite):** An email marketing platform designed for e-commerce businesses, now part of Oracle NetSuite's suite of cloud business management tools.

8. **Citrix (Cloud Software Group):** A multinational tech company that provides workspace, networking, and analytics solutions to enable secure remote work and collaboration.

9. **Nexcom Digital Solutions:** A digital transformation company offering technology solutions and services to businesses across various industries.

WORKPLACE COMPETENCIES:

1	Customer Focus	Ability to anticipate, understand, and respond to the needs of customers, ensuring high levels of satisfaction.
2	Collaboration	Working effectively with cross-functional teams and stakeholders to optimize customer relationship strategies and achieve common goals.
3	Technological Proficiency	Demonstrating expertise in CRM platforms and related software to manage and analyze customer interactions efficiently.
4	Analytical Thinking	Using data-driven insights to identify trends, make informed decisions, and improve customer engagement strategies.
5	Project Management	Managing multiple customer-related tasks and projects simultaneously, ensuring timely completion and quality outcomes.

PERSONAL COMPETENCIES:

1	Adaptability	Adjusting quickly to new technologies, customer needs, and evolving market trends in a fast-paced industry.
2	Integrity	Upholding ethical standards and ensuring the confidentiality and security of customer data.
3	Emotional Intelligence	Understanding and managing personal emotions while empathizing with others to build strong customer relationships.
4	Problem-Solving	Quickly identifying customer challenges and developing effective solutions to enhance satisfaction.
5	Continuous Learning	Staying updated on CRM tools, strategies, and market developments to remain competitive and innovative in the field.

KEY KNOWLEDGE, SKILLS, AND ABILITIES:

KNOWLEDGE	SKILLS	ABILITIES
Familiarity with customer engagement strategies, CRM platforms (e.g., Salesforce or Microsoft Dynamics), and data analytics.	Communication, data analysis, customer service, and CRM software proficiency.	Strategic thinking, adaptability to new technology, and ability to interpret data for business decisions.

RECOMMENDED HIGH SCHOOL COURSES TO PREPARE FOR A CAREER IN CUSTOMER RELATIONSHIP MANAGEMENT:

1	**Business Essentials**	This course introduces business concepts, including customer relations.
2	**Digital Marketing**	This course familiarizes students with online marketing techniques crucial for CRM roles.
3	**Information Technology**	This course teaches basic IT skills for CRM software and data management.
4	**Statistics**	This course helps students develop analytical thinking and familiarity with data, which are key in CRM roles.
5	**Communication/Public Speaking**	This course enhances verbal and written communication skills essential for customer engagement and support.

TOP 10 OCCUPATIONS IN CUSTOMER RELATIONSHIP MANAGEMENT:

Rank	Occupation	Education/Training	Average Wage
1	CRM Manager	Bachelor's degree in business, marketing, or IT; CRM platform certifications.	$85,000–$105,000 per year
2	Salesforce Administrator	Bachelor's degree in information systems; salesforce certifications	$75,000–$95,000 per year
3	CRM Data Analyst	Bachelor's degree in data analytics or business analytics.	$65,000–$85,000 per year
4	Customer Success Manager	Bachelor's degree in business or communication; experience with CRM software.	$70,000–$90,000 per year
5	Digital Marketing Specialist	Bachelor's degree in marketing or digital media.	$60,000–$80,000 per year
6	CRM Developer	Bachelor's degree in computer science; experience with CRM application programming interfaces (APIs).	$95,000–$120,000 per year
7	Business Analyst (CRM)	Bachelor's degree in business administration or IT.	$70,000–$95,000 per year
8	Technical Support Specialist (CRM)	Associate's or bachelor's degree in IT.	$55,000–$70,000 per year
9	Product Manager (CRM Software)	Bachelor's or master's degree in business or product management.	$90,000–$120,000 per year
10	CRM Consultant	Bachelor's degree in business or IT; CRM platform certifications.	$85,000–$110,000 per year

MY NOTES:

CAREER PATHWAYS

DIGITAL MARKETING

Explore
MY PATH

INDUSTRY OVERVIEW:

Let's talk about digital marketing in North Carolina! It's basically the cool kid on the business block right now, helping all sorts of companies—from tiny startups to big corporate players—get noticed online. We're talking social media, emails, search engines, websites … the whole digital shebang.

With everyone and their grandma shopping online these days, businesses are scrambling to catch people's attention on their phones and laptops. It's all about that digital life now, which is super important for pretty much every industry out there.

GROWTH PROJECTIONS:

Now, here's the exciting part—this digital marketing scene is growing faster than a viral TikTok dance! Experts are saying it's going to expand by about 7%–9% each year in North Carolina. Why? Companies are all about that personalized touch now. They want ads that feel like they're talking just to you, based on all that data they've collected. Plus, they're trying to make your online shopping experience smoother than ever. This means tons of opportunities are popping up for people who know their way around the digital world. So, if you're into tech or creativity or just love the idea of shaping how people interact online, the digital marketing world in North Carolina might be your perfect playground. The future's looking bright!

TYPES OF PRODUCTS AND SERVICES PRODUCED IN DIGITAL MARKETING IN NORTH CAROLINA:

Search engine optimization (SEO): Strategies to improve a website's visibility and ranking in search engine results pages.

Content marketing: Development and distribution of valuable, relevant content to attract and retain a target audience.

Email marketing: Design and execution of targeted email campaigns to nurture leads and maintain customer relationships.

Analytics and reporting: Tracking, analyzing, and reporting on digital marketing performance metrics to inform strategy.

Influencer marketing: Collaboration with influential individuals in specific niches to promote products or services to their followers.

DIGITAL MARKETING COMPANIES IN NORTH CAROLINA:

1. **Red Ventures:** A multifaceted digital marketing and technology company that owns and operates various online brands and businesses.

2. **Walk West:** A full-service digital marketing agency based in Raleigh, NC, offering services such as web design, content creation, and brand strategy.

3. **Atlantic BT:** A technology consulting firm specializing in custom software development, digital transformation, and managed IT services.

4. **Rivers Agency:** A creative advertising and digital marketing agency known for its integrated approach to branding and communications.

5. **Union:** A digital product agency that focuses on designing and developing web and mobile applications for various industries.

6. **Go Fish Digital:** An online marketing agency specializing in SEO, reputation management, and content marketing.

7. **The Republik:** An independent advertising agency that provides creative services, media planning, and brand strategies to diverse clients.

8. **Meridian Group:** A full-service marketing and public relations firm offering integrated communications solutions to businesses and organizations.

9. **MicroMass Communications:** A healthcare communications agency that specializes in developing behavior-change strategies and patient engagement programs.

10. **Tactic:** A digital marketing agency that focuses on data-driven strategies, including paid media, SEO, and analytics.

WORKPLACE COMPETENCIES:

1	Collaboration and Teamwork	Working in multidisciplinary teams that include content creators, data analysts, and designers.
2	Proficiency	Expertise in digital tools, such as Google Ads, social media platforms, and content management systems.
3	Project Management	Handling multiple campaigns, managing deadlines, and ensuring client expectations are met.
4	Client Focus	Understanding client needs and delivering tailored marketing strategies.
5	Data-Driven Decision-Making	Using analytics to guide marketing strategies and optimize performance.

PERSONAL COMPETENCIES:

1	Adaptability	Ability to stay up-to-date with rapidly changing digital marketing trends.
2	Creativity	Innovating in content creation and digital campaign strategies.
3	Problem-Solving	Addressing campaign challenges quickly and effectively.
4	Ethics and Integrity	Maintaining transparency in marketing efforts and adhering to ethical standards.
5	Continuous Learning	Staying current with the latest digital tools, strategies, and industry developments.

KEY KNOWLEDGE, SKILLS, AND ABILITIES:

KNOWLEDGE	SKILLS	ABILITIES
In-depth understanding of digital advertising, social media algorithms, SEO best practices, content marketing techniques, and data analytics tools.	Proficiency in Google Analytics, SEO tools (e.g., SEMrush), social media management tools (e.g., Hootsuite), content creation, and data-driven decision-making.	Strong ability to adapt to digital marketing trends, analyze performance metrics, collaborate across teams, and execute creative marketing campaigns.

RECOMMENDED HIGH SCHOOL COURSES TO PREPARE FOR A CAREER IN DIGITAL MARKETING:

1	Introduction to Marketing	This course provides foundational knowledge in marketing principles and strategies.
2	Graphic Design	This course teaches visual communication skills essential to creating digital content.
3	Web Design and Development	This course offers basic skills in designing and managing websites—crucial for digital marketing.
4	Business and Technology	This course introduces students to the business principles and technology tools used in marketing.
5	Digital Media/Multimedia	This course focuses on the creation of digital content, such as videos, graphics, and social media posts, which are key components of digital marketing.

TOP 10 OCCUPATIONS IN DIGITAL MARKETING:

Rank	Occupation	Education/Training	Average Wage
1	Digital Marketing Manager	Bachelor's degree in marketing, communications, or business.	$75,000–$95,000 per year
2	SEO Specialist	Bachelor's degree in marketing or IT; SEO tool certifications.	$55,000–$70,000 per year
3	Social Media Manager	Bachelor's degree in communications or marketing; social media platform certifications.	$50,000–$70,000 per year
4	Content Marketing Manager	Bachelor's degree in journalism, English, or marketing.	$65,000–$85,000 per year
5	PPC Specialist (Pay-per-click Specialist)	Bachelor's degree in marketing; Google Ads certification.	$60,000–$80,000 per year
6	Email Marketing Specialist	Bachelor's degree in marketing; email marketing tool certifications.	$50,000–$65,000 per year
7	User Experience / User Interface (UX / UI) Designer	Bachelor's degree in design; UX/UI experience.	$75,000–$95,000 per year
8	Digital Analyst	Bachelor's degree in data analytics, marketing, or business.	$60,000–$75,000 per year
9	Graphic Designer (Digital)	Bachelor's degree in graphic design; proficiency in Adobe Creative Suite.	$45,000–$60,000 per year
10	Digital Strategist	Bachelor's degree in business or marketing; digital strategy experience.	$70,000–$90,000 per year

MY NOTES:

SECTION 11

CAREER PATHWAYS

ENERGY

INDUSTRY OVERVIEW:

North Carolina has gone from making old-school stuff like tobacco and textiles to becoming the superheroes of advanced energy, leading the way with solar panels, electric cars, and lithium batteries. By 2030, the energy industry here is set to explode (in the best way), with solar farms and EV chargers popping up everywhere, creating thousands of jobs. Companies are pouring billions into the state, knowing it's the hotspot for clean energy innovation. From wind turbines to smart grids, North Carolina is the place to be if you want to save the planet, make bank, and be part of the future.

GROWTH PROJECTIONS:

North Carolina is at the forefront of the clean energy revolution, with significant investments in renewable energy, electric vehicle (EV) infrastructure, and energy efficiency technologies. The energy industry in North Carolina is projected to grow substantially, driven by state and federal commitments to clean energy goals. Between 2021 and 2030, the state anticipates substantial job growth in this sector, particularly in roles related to electric vehicles, battery manufacturing, and renewable energy production.

TYPES OF PRODUCTS AND SERVICES PRODUCED IN THE ENERGY INDUSTRY IN NORTH CAROLINA:

Solar panels and photovoltaic systems: Harnessing sunlight to generate clean, renewable electricity for homes, businesses, and beyond.

Lithium batteries: High-capacity storage solutions that power everything from smartphones to electric vehicles.

Smart grid technology: Advanced systems optimizing energy distribution for reliable and sustainable power delivery.

Energy efficiency consulting: Expert guidance to reduce energy consumption and lower costs for businesses and households.

Advanced HVAC systems: Innovative climate control technologies for maximum energy efficiency and comfort.

ENERGY COMPANIES IN NORTH CAROLINA:

1. **Duke Energy:** North Carolina's largest utility provider, delivering reliable electricity while investing heavily in renewable energy and grid modernization.

2. **Siemens:** A company supporting the state's energy sector with advanced technology solutions for power generation, automation, and smart grid innovations.

3. **Toyota:** A multinational automotive manufacturer revolutionizing clean transportation in North Carolina by advancing electric vehicle production and developing innovative battery technologies.

4. **GE Renewable Energy:** A company driving North Carolina's green energy transition through wind turbines, solar technology, and sustainable power solutions.

5. **NextEra Energy:** A leader in renewable energy, developing large-scale solar farms and wind projects across the state.

6. **SAS Institute:** A company based in Cary, NC, that supports the energy sector by providing data analytics solutions to optimize energy efficiency and sustainability strategies.

7. **ABB:** A company empowering the state's energy future with cutting-edge technology in automation, electrification, and EV charging infrastructure.

8. **Strata Clean Energy**: A North Carolina–based company specializing in the development, construction, and operation of utility-scale solar farms.

9. **Cree (Wolfspeed):** A company leading the charge in silicon carbide technology for energy-efficient electronics and renewable energy systems in the state.

10. **Eaton Corporation**: A company enhancing North Carolina's energy landscape by providing advanced power management solutions and smart energy technologies.

WORKPLACE COMPETENCIES:

1	**Problem-Solving**	Identifying and implementing effective solutions to complex energy sector challenges.
2	**Collaboration**	Working seamlessly with cross-functional teams to deliver successful energy projects.
3	**Time Management**	Prioritizing tasks and meeting deadlines in dynamic energy environments.
4	**Adaptability**	Adjusting to evolving technologies, regulations, and market trends in the energy sector.

PERSONAL COMPETENCIES:

1	**Dependability**	Consistently delivering quality work and meeting commitments in the energy industry.
2	**Initiative**	Proactively identifying opportunities and driving improvements in energy processes.
3	**Continuous Learning**	Staying current with advancements and acquiring new skills to enhance expertise in energy solutions.
4	**Resilience**	Maintaining focus and determination in the face of challenges and industry shifts.

KEY KNOWLEDGE, SKILLS, AND ABILITIES:

KNOWLEDGE	SKILLS	ABILITIES
Understanding of renewable and nonrenewable energy systems; familiarity with OSHA and energy compliance standards; and knowledge of green technologies and their applications.	Analyzing energy data to solve complex problems; operating and maintaining energy systems and machinery; and managing timelines, resources, and budgets for energy projects.	Ability to work with energy equipment and systems and explain technical details to nonspecialists..

RECOMMENDED HIGH SCHOOL COURSES TO PREPARE FOR A CAREER IN ENERGY:

1	Physics	This course provides a foundation in energy principles, mechanics, and electricity, which are critical for understanding energy systems and technologies.
2	Mathematics (Algebra, Geometry, and Pre-Calculus)	Mathematics courses help develop the problem-solving skills and analytical thinking necessary for energy engineering, technology, and data analysis roles.
3	Environmental Science	This course introduces students to renewable energy, sustainability, and the environmental impact of energy production and consumption.
4	Engineering or Technology Education	This course offers hands-on experience with design, robotics, and energy systems, preparing students for technical and engineering roles.
5	Computer Science or Programming	This course equips students with skills in coding and software tools used in energy modeling, smart grids, and renewable energy technologies.

TOP 10 OCCUPATIONS IN ENERGY:

Rank	Occupation	Education/Training	Average Wage
1	**Energy Engineer**	Bachelor's degree in engineering (mechanical, electrical, or a related field); professional engineer (PE) license preferred.	$71,305–$96,408 per year
2	**Energy Efficiency Specialist**	Bachelor's degree in environmental science, engineering, or a related field; certifications such as Certified Energy Manager (CEM) advantageous.	$75,604–$89,064 per year
3	**Energy Analyst/ Auditor**	Bachelor's degree in engineering, environmental science, or a related discipline; experience in energy auditing preferred.	$67,299–$93,022 per year
4	**Electrical Power Engineer**	Bachelor's degree in electrical engineering; professional engineer (PE) license often required.	$146,692–$172,921 per year
5	**Renewable Energy Technician**	Associate's degree or technical certification in renewable energy technology or a related field.	$40,000–$60,000 per year
6	**HVAC Technician**	Postsecondary certificate or associate's degree in HVAC technology; state licensure may be required.	$45,000–$65,000 per year
7	**Solar Photovoltaic Installer**	High school diploma; technical training or certification in solar installation preferred.	$40,000–$50,000 per year
8	**Wind Turbine Technician**	Associate's degree in wind energy technology or related field; certifications may enhance job prospects.	$50,000–$70,000 per year
9	**Energy Manager**	Bachelor's degree in engineering, business, or a related field; certified energy manager (CEM) credential preferred.	$90,000–$115,000 per year
10	**Environmental Scientist**	Bachelor's degree in environmental science or a related discipline; advanced degrees may be beneficial.	$60,000–$80,000 per year

MY NOTES:

CAREER PATHWAYS

FINANCIAL PLANNING

Explore
MY PATH

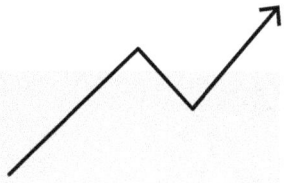

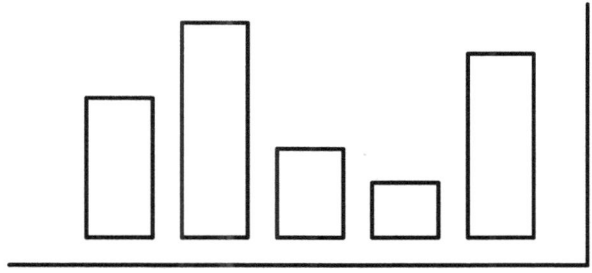

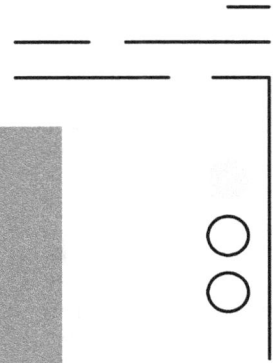

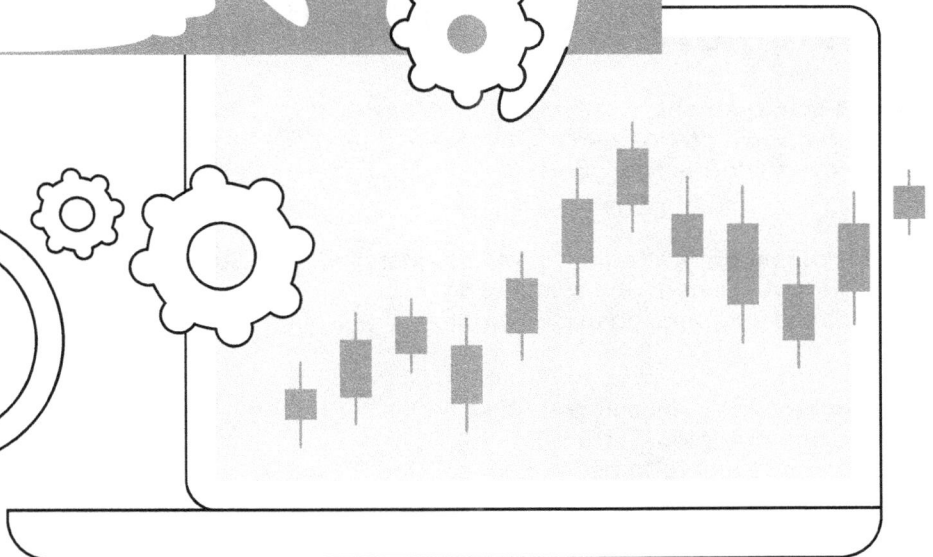

INDUSTRY OVERVIEW:

Hey there, future money bosses! Let's talk about the financial planning scene in North Carolina. Picture this: You've got all these cool cats helping people figure out what to do with their cash, investments, and retirement dreams. It's like having a money coach but for your whole life! Charlotte's where it's at—this place is like the Wall Street of North Carolina, no joke. These financial planners are the real MVPs, showing folks how to make their money work for them, whether it's budgeting for that sweet new ride or ensuring they're not eating ramen in their golden years. More and more people are realizing they need a pro to help them navigate the money maze, so these planners are kind of a big deal in North Carolina's financial world.

GROWTH PROJECTIONS:

Now, let's peek into the crystal ball for this industry. Spoiler alert: It's looking pretty sweet! With all the boomers hitting retirement age and the stock market acting crazier than a cat on catnip, people need financial advice more than ever. According to the North Carolina Department of Commerce, the industry is expected to grow about 5% through 2032, which is not too shabby. But here's the cool part—it's not just your grandpa's financial planning anymore. We're talking robo-advisors and digital services that make managing your money as easy as swiping right on your crush. So, if you're thinking about a career where you can help people and play with numbers, financial planning just might be your jam!

TYPES OF PRODUCTS AND SERVICES PRODUCED IN FINANCIAL PLANNING IN NORTH CAROLINA:

Investment management: Customized portfolio creation and ongoing management to help clients achieve their financial goals.

Retirement planning: Strategies to ensure financial security during retirement years, including 401(k) guidance and pension optimization.

Estate planning: Assistance in creating wills, trusts, and other legal structures to efficiently transfer assets to beneficiaries.

Business succession planning: Guidance for business owners on transferring ownership or selling their companies.

Risk management: Identification and mitigation of potential financial risks through diversification and appropriate asset allocation.

FINANCIAL PLANNING COMPANIES IN NORTH CAROLINA:

1. **Bank of America:** A multinational investment bank and financial services company headquartered in Charlotte, NC, offering a wide range of banking, investing, asset management, and other financial and risk management products and services.

2. **Truist Financial Corporation:** A bank holding company formed in 2019 through the merger of BB&T and SunTrust Banks; headquartered in Charlotte, NC, providing various banking and financial services.

3. **Vanguard:** An American registered investment advisor known for its low-cost mutual funds and exchange-traded funds, headquartered in Malvern, PA.

4. **Edward Jones:** A financial services firm headquartered in St Louis, MO, focusing on providing personalized investment advice and services to individual investors.

5. **Northwestern Mutual:** A Milwaukee-based financial services organization that provides life insurance, disability income insurance, long-term care insurance, and investment products and services.

6. **Fidelity Investments:** A multinational financial services corporation based in Boston, MA, offering a wide range of investment products, including mutual funds, brokerage services, and retirement services.

7. **CAPTRUST:** An independent investment research and fee-based advisory firm headquartered in Raleigh, NC, providing investment advisory services for institutional investors, private investors, and corporate retirement plans.

8. **MassMutual Carolinas:** A general agency of Massachusetts Mutual Life Insurance Company (MassMutual) offering insurance and financial products and services in the Carolinas region.

9. **Principal Financial Group:** A global financial investment management and insurance company headquartered in Des Moines, IA, providing retirement, insurance, and asset management solutions.

10. **Truist Investment Services:** The investment services arm of Truist Financial Corporation, offering various investment and wealth management services to individual and institutional clients.

WORKPLACE COMPETENCIES:

1	Client Focus	Understanding client needs and developing customized financial plans.
2	Ethical Conduct	Maintaining fiduciary responsibility and prioritizing client interests.
3	Problem-Solving	Analyzing financial data to provide tailored solutions.
4	Technological Proficiency	Using financial planning software and tools.
5	Time Management	Balancing multiple clients and administrative tasks.

PERSONAL COMPETENCIES:

1	Attention to Detail	Precision in developing financial plans to avoid errors.
2	Adaptability	Flexibility in adjusting strategies based on market changes.
3	Communication	Effectively explaining financial concepts to clients.
4	Continuous Learning	Staying updated on market trends, regulations, and financial products.
5	Integrity	Adhering to ethical guidelines and ensuring client trust.

KEY KNOWLEDGE, SKILLS, AND ABILITIES:

KNOWLEDGE	SKILLS	ABILITIES
Familiarity with financial products, tax-advantaged investments, retirement accounts, and estate planning strategies.	Analytical skills for data and financial markets, communication skills for client management, and strategic financial planning.	Ability to forecast market trends, build long-term client relationships, and manage complex portfolios.

RECOMMENDED HIGH SCHOOL COURSES TO PREPARE FOR A CAREER IN FINANCIAL PLANNING:

1	**Mathematics (Algebra, Calculus, and Statistics)**	These courses provide a strong foundation of mathematical skills, which are essential for analyzing financial data, budgeting, and forecasting.
2	**Economics**	This course teaches students economic principles to aid in analyzing financial markets and understanding investment strategies.
3	**Business and Personal Finance**	This course exposes students to personal financial management, budgeting, and investment planning, which are critical for foundational knowledge.
4	**Accounting**	This course introduces students to basic accounting principles, which are essential to understanding financial statements, budgeting, and tax strategies.
5	**Computer Science or Technology**	These courses familiarize students with financial software and tools, which are essential in the modern financial planning industry.

TOP 10 OCCUPATIONS IN FINANCIAL PLANNING:

Rank	Occupation	Education/Training	Average Wage
1	Personal Financial Advisor	Bachelor's degree in finance, business, or economics; CFP certification recommended.	$70,000–$120,000 per year
2	Certified Financial Planner (CFP)	Bachelor's degree in a related field; CFP certification required.	$75,000–$125,000 per year
3	Investment Advisor	Bachelor's degree in finance or economics; Series 7 and 66 licenses often required.	$60,000–$100,000 per year
4	Wealth Manager	Bachelor's degree in finance or business; CFP or CFA (Chartered Financial Analyst) certifications recommended.	$80,000–$150,000 per year
5	Portfolio Manager	Bachelor's or master's degree in finance, business, or economics; CFA certification typically required.	$90,000–$150,000 per year
6	Financial Analyst	Bachelor's degree in finance, accounting, or economics; CFA certification is often pursued.	$65,000–$110,000 per year
7	Estate Planner	Bachelor's degree in law, finance, or business; CFP or related certifications recommended.	$70,000–$120,000 per year
8	Insurance Advisor	Bachelor's degree in finance, business, or insurance; relevant state licensure required.	$60,000–$100,000 per year
9	Retirement Planning Consultant	Bachelor's degree in finance or economics; CFP or relevant retirement planning certifications recommended.	$65,000–$110,000 per year
10	Tax Advisor	Bachelor's degree in accounting, finance, or law; CPA certification or Enrolled Agent (EA) status often required.	$70,000–$120,000 per year

MY NOTES:

SECTION 13

CAREER PATHWAYS

GAME ART
DESIGN

Explore
MY PATH

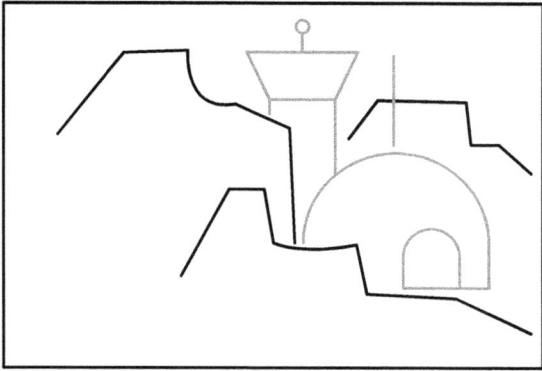

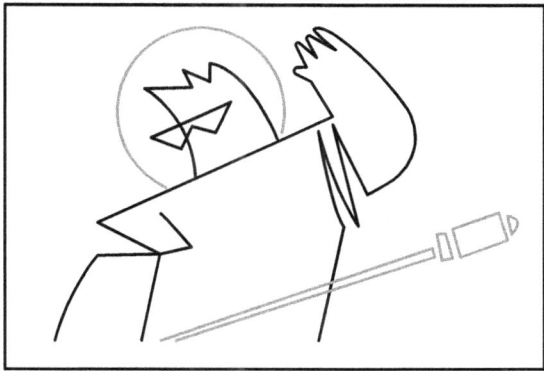

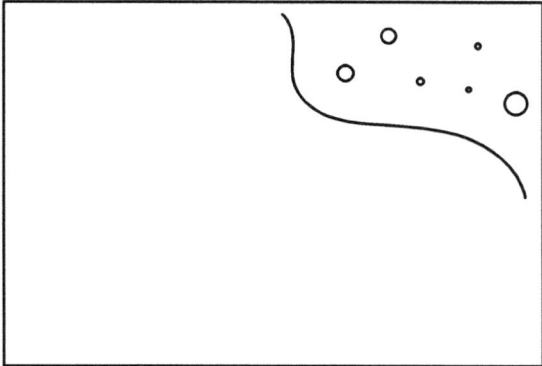

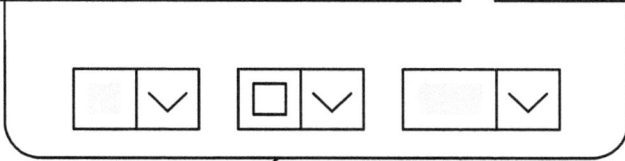

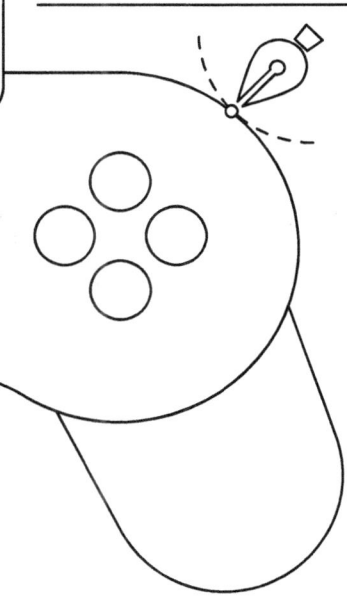

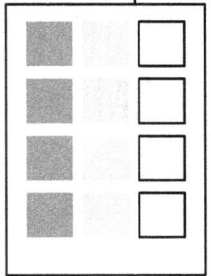

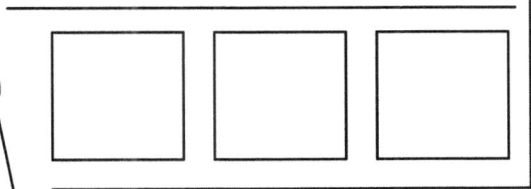

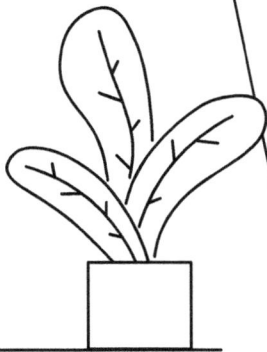

INDUSTRY OVERVIEW:

North Carolina's game design scene is totally blowing up right now. We've got indie developers and big-name studios setting up shop all over the state, which means the industry is growing like crazy. Game artists are the cool cats who create all the eye candy you see in video games—characters, environments, special effects, you name it! And with AR and VR tech taking off, game artists are in higher demand than ever. North Carolina's become a hotspot for game design and interactive media companies, so if you're into art and gaming, this is the place to be!

GROWTH PROJECTIONS:

Looking ahead, things are only getting better for game artists in North Carolina. According to the state's Department of Commerce, the industry is expected to grow by 5%–7% each year for the next 10 years. That's huge! But what's driving this growth? Game tech is constantly evolving, giving artists new tools to create mind-blowing visuals.

Plus, esports are becoming mega-popular, creating even more opportunities for game artists. And it's not just about entertainment anymore—educational games are on the rise, too. So, if you're thinking about a career in game art, now's the time to jump in. The future's looking bright and pixelated!

TYPES OF PRODUCTS AND SERVICES PRODUCED IN GAME ART DESIGN IN NORTH CAROLINA:

3D character models: Detailed digital representations of game characters, including their appearance and animations.

Environmental design: Creation of immersive game worlds, landscapes, and architectural elements.

Concept art: Initial visual representations of characters, environments, and objects to guide the game's artistic direction.

User interface (UI) design: Development of intuitive and visually appealing menus, heads-up displays, and other onscreen elements.

Animation services: Creation of fluid and lifelike movements for characters and objects within the game.

GAME ART DESIGN COMPANIES IN NORTH CAROLINA:

1. **Epic Games:** A major American video game and software developer known for creating the Unreal Engine and popular games like *Fortnite* and *Gears of War*.

2. **Red Storm Entertainment:** A video game developer founded by author Tom Clancy, known for tactical shooter games and the *Rainbow Six* series.

3. **Insomniac Games:** A renowned game studio famous for developing the *Ratchet & Clank* series, *Spyro the Dragon*, and Marvel's Spider-Man games.

4. **Funcom:** A Norwegian video game developer and publisher, known for online games like *Anarchy Online* and *The Secret World*.

5. **Psyonix:** The studio behind the popular vehicular soccer game *Rocket League*, later acquired by Epic Games.

6. **Imangi Studios:** A small independent game developer best known for creating the mobile game *Temple Run*.

7. **Voltaku Studios:** A relatively new studio focused on creating narrative-driven experiences and interactive storytelling.

8. **Spark Plug Games:** An independent game developer based in North Carolina, creating games for various platforms, including mobile and VR.

9. **Little Green Men Games:** An indie game studio known for developing space simulation games like *Starpoint Gemini*.

10. *The Escapist*: An online magazine covering video games, movies, TV shows, and other aspects of geek culture (not a game developer like the other companies on this list).

WORKPLACE COMPETENCIES:

1	Collaboration	Ability to work effectively with diverse teams, including designers, programmers, and project managers, to achieve common goals.
2	Project Management	Skilled in organizing and managing tasks, resources, and timelines to ensure game development projects are completed successfully.
3	Technical Proficiency	Expertise in using software and tools like Unreal Engine, Blender, and Adobe Creative Suite to create and refine game assets.
4	Problem-Solving	Ability to address technical and creative challenges efficiently during the design and development process.
5	Adaptability	Flexibility to embrace and learn new technologies, trends, and workflows in a rapidly evolving industry.

PERSONAL COMPETENCIES:

1	Creativity	A strong imagination and originality to conceptualize and produce unique game designs and visual elements.
2	Attention to Detail	Precision and thoroughness in creating high-quality assets and ensuring design consistency.
3	Time Management	Ability to prioritize tasks and meet deadlines in a fast-paced production environment.
4	Critical Thinking	Logical reasoning to evaluate design decisions and optimize gameplay experiences.
5	Continuous Learning	A commitment to staying updated with industry advancements, tools, and trends to maintain relevance and expertise.

KEY KNOWLEDGE, SKILLS, AND ABILITIES:

KNOWLEDGE	SKILLS	ABILITIES
Familiarity with game design principles, 3D modeling, game engines, storytelling, lighting, and animation.	Proficiency in digital art software character design, texture creation, and 3D environment rendering.	Strong creative vision, problem-solving, attention to detail, and ability to work in teams.

RECOMMENDED HIGH SCHOOL COURSES TO PREPARE FOR A CAREER IN GAME ART DESIGN:

1	**Art and Design**	This course introduces the principles of art, color theory, and design, which form the foundation for concept art and visual design.
2	**Digital Media/Multimedia**	Such courses focus on creating digital content using software like Photoshop and Illustrator to develop basic digital art skills.
3	**Computer Science**	This course introduces fundamental programming knowledge, which is crucial for understanding how game engines work.
4	**3D Modeling/Animation**	This course introduces modeling or animation using tools such as Blender or Maya.
5	**Mathematics (Algebra and Geometry)**	These courses are essential to understanding spatial relationships and physics in game design.

TOP 10 OCCUPATIONS IN GAME ART DESIGN:

Rank	Occupation	Education/Training	Average Wage
1	3D Modeler	Bachelor's degree in 3D modeling or a related field.	$55,000–$70,000
2	Game Designer	Bachelor's degree in game design or interactive media.	$60,000–$85,000
3	Concept Artist	Bachelor's degree in fine arts or digital illustration.	$50,000–$75,000
4	Character Animator	Bachelor's degree in animation or digital arts.	$55,000–$80,000
5	Environment Artist	Bachelor's degree in digital arts or environmental design.	$55,000–$75,000
6	Technical Artist	Bachelor's degree in game design or computer graphics.	$65,000–$90,000
7	UI Artist	Bachelor's degree in graphic design or game art.	$55,000–$75,000
8	VFX Artist (visual effects)	Bachelor's degree in VFX or digital arts.	$60,000–$85,000
9	Level Designer	Bachelor's degree in game design or interactive design.	$55,000–$75,000
10	Texture Artist	Bachelor's degree in digital arts or game art.	$50,000–$70,000

MY NOTES:

SECTION 14

CAREER PATHWAYS

GRAPHIC DESIGN

INDUSTRY OVERVIEW:

So, graphic design is a pretty big deal in North Carolina! It's all about making things look good and work well, whether that's for ads, video games, websites, or social media posts. These days, since everyone's shopping and hanging out online, companies really need designers who can make their stuff stand out and be easy to use. Designers use different computer programs to create cool visuals that catch people's attention and get the message across—kind of like how TikTok and Instagram need to look appealing to keep people interested. They work on all sorts of things, from coming up with brand logos and building websites to creating animations and designing apps that people actually want to use.

GROWTH PROJECTIONS:

The graphic design scene is looking pretty solid right now—it's growing about 6% each year since everyone's hungry for more digital content. If you're into design, you might want to check out cities like Raleigh, Durham, or Charlotte, since they're full of tech companies that need help with their social media posts, marketing stuff, phone apps, and overall brand look. These companies are always seeking fresh talent to make their online presence pop!

TYPES OF PRODUCTS AND SERVICES PRODUCED IN GRAPHIC DESIGN IN NORTH CAROLINA:

Branding packages: Development of comprehensive brand identities, including logos, color schemes, typography, and style guides.

Print materials: Design of brochures, flyers, business cards, and other physical marketing collateral.

Website design: Creation of visually appealing and user-friendly websites for businesses and organizations.

Social media graphics: Production of eye-catching images and designs for various social media platforms.

Infographic design: Transformation of complex data and information into visually engaging and easily understandable graphics.

GRAPHIC DESIGN COMPANIES IN NORTH CAROLINA:

1. **McKinney:** A major advertising and design agency headquartered in Durham, NC, and working with national brands like Nike and Samsung.

2. **Luquire:** A Charlotte-based strategic communications and design firm serving clients nationwide, with a strong Southeast presence.

3. **Red Hat Creative:** An in-house design team for Red Hat in Raleigh, NC influencing tech industry design trends nationally.

4. **Capstrat (now Ketchum):** A Raleigh-based design and communications firm serving national clients, owned by global giant Ketchum.

5. **Adobe:** A national company that is headquartered in California but maintains a creative hub in Research Triangle Park.

6. **Wray Ward:** A Charlotte-based creative firm working with national home and building brands.

7. **Clean Design:** A Raleigh-based agency serving national clients across various industries.

8. **The Variable:** A Winston-Salem–based agency working with national brands like Lowes Foods and P&G.

9. **McCann (MRM):** A global agency with operations in Charlotte, NC serving major national brands.

10. **Mythic:** A Charlotte-based full-service agency working with national and international clients.

WORKPLACE COMPETENCIES:

1	Collaboration and Teamwork	Ability to work effectively in diverse teams to achieve shared goals and deliver cohesive design solutions.
2	Project Management	Skilled in managing time, resources, and milestones to ensure project completion within deadlines and budget.
3	Technological Proficiency	Competence in using industry-standard design software and digital tools to create high-quality work.
4	Client Communication	Strong ability to understand client needs, present design concepts, and incorporate feedback effectively.
5	Attention to Detail	Ensuring precision in all aspects of design, from typography to color consistency, to deliver polished results.

PERSONAL COMPETENCIES:

1	Adaptability	Ability to adjust quickly to changing project demands, technology advancements, and client preferences.
2	Creativity	A talent for generating innovative design ideas and solutions that captivate and communicate effectively.
3	Continuous Learning	Commitment to staying updated on design trends, tools, and industry best practices to maintain a competitive edge.
4	Critical Thinking	Ability to analyze project requirements and challenges to develop strategic, effective design solutions.
5	Resilience	Maintaining a positive attitude and persistence in the face of feedback, revisions, or tight deadlines.

KEY KNOWLEDGE, SKILLS, AND ABILITIES:

KNOWLEDGE	SKILLS	ABILITIES
Familiarity with typography, branding, color theory, layout principles, user-centered design, and digital marketing concepts.	Mastery of Adobe Creative Suite, strong drawing and conceptualization skills, proficiency in web design, and ability to use wireframing tools.	Strong creative problem-solving, attention to detail, ability to communicate visually, and ability to handle feedback and effectively make revisions.

RECOMMENDED HIGH SCHOOL COURSES TO PREPARE FOR A CAREER IN GRAPHIC DESIGN:

1	**Graphic Design and Digital Arts**	This course provides an introduction to graphic design principles, digital illustration, and tools like Adobe Photoshop and Illustrator.
2	**Web Design and Development**	This course introduces the basics of web design, HTML, CSS, and web development concepts, along with design principles for UX/UI.
3	**Multimedia Arts**	This course focuses on multimedia content creation, including video, animation, and motion graphics.
4	**Marketing and Branding**	This course teaches foundational marketing strategies and branding concepts, which are crucial for roles in branding and advertising.
5	**Art and Design Foundations**	This course is focused on fundamental artistic skills, including drawing, color theory, and composition, which are essential for all forms of visual design.

TOP 10 OCCUPATIONS IN GRAPHIC DESIGN:

Rank	Occupation	Education/Training	Average Wage
1	Graphic Designer	Bachelor's degree in graphic design, digital arts, or a related field.	$52,000 per year
2	UI Designer	Bachelor's degree in web design, human–computer interaction, or a related field.	$70,000 per year
3	UX Designer	Bachelor's degree in graphic design, psychology, or human-centered design.	$78,000 per year
4	Web Designer	Bachelor's degree in web design, multimedia, or a related field.	$62,000 per year
5	Motion Graphics Designer	Bachelor's degree in animation, multimedia, or digital arts.	$65,000 per year
6	Art Director	Bachelor's degree in fine arts, graphic design, or a related field.	$85,000 per year
7	Digital Illustrator	Bachelor's degree in graphic arts or illustration.	$56,000 per year
8	Brand Designer	Bachelor's degree in marketing, graphic design, or a related field.	$60,000 per year
9	Creative Director	Bachelor's or master's degree in design, art, or marketing.	$95,000 per year
10	Visual Designer	Bachelor's degree in graphic design or a related field.	$68,000 per year

MY NOTES:

SECTION 15

CAREER PATHWAYS

HORTICULTURE

Explore
MY PATH

INDUSTRY OVERVIEW:

Did you know North Carolina's horticulture scene is kind of a big deal? It's not just about pretty flowers—we're talking fruits, veggies, landscaping, and even greenhouse stuff. The state's got this awesome mix of climates and soils that make it perfect for growing all sorts of plants. We're actually up there with the best states for growing flowers and nursery plants, thanks to all the folks wanting to spruce up their yards and businesses. Whether it's running a nursery, growing crops in greenhouses, or making spaces look pretty with ornamental plants, there's a lot going on in North Carolina's plant world.

GROWTH PROJECTIONS:

The future's looking pretty sweet for the state's horticulture industry. People are getting more into eco-friendly gardening and landscaping, which is great news for the plant biz. As cities keep growing, more people want green spaces and nice landscapes. The cool thing is that there's this whole trend of sustainable and eco-friendly gardening that's really taking off. This means more jobs for plant experts—plus, all the new tech in farming is making everything more efficient. The industry's expected to grow by about 5%–7% over the next 10 years, so if you're into plants, horticulture might be a pretty solid career move!

TYPES OF PRODUCTS AND SERVICES PRODUCED IN HORTICULTURE IN NORTH CAROLINA:

Nursery plants: A wide variety of trees, shrubs, and ornamental plants grown for landscaping and gardening purposes.

Greenhouse vegetables: Tomatoes, cucumbers, peppers, and leafy greens produced year-round in controlled environments.

Christmas trees: Farm-grown evergreen trees for holiday decorations, with North Carolina being a major producer.

Landscape design services: Professional planning and implementation of outdoor spaces for residential and commercial properties.

Horticultural consulting: Professional services for pest management, soil analysis, and crop optimization for commercial growers.

HORTICULTURE COMPANIES IN NORTH CAROLINA:

1. **Metrolina Greenhouses:** One of the largest single-site heated greenhouse operations in the US, located in Huntersville, NC; it's known for producing annuals, perennials, and holiday plants.

2. **Hoffman Nursery:** A company located in Rougemont, NC, specializing in ornamental and native grasses, sedges, and rushes and supplying wholesale plants to the horticulture industry.

3. **Plant Delights Nursery:** A specialty mail-order nursery in Raleigh, NC, known for rare and unusual perennials; founded by plant expert Tony Avent.

4. **Scott Farms:** A family-owned farm in Lucama, NC, specializing in sweet potatoes and known for sustainable farming practices and global distribution.

5. **Fairview Greenhouses & Garden Center:** A retail garden center in Raleigh, NC, offering a wide variety of plants, gardening supplies, and landscaping services.

6. **Camellia Forest Nursery:** A nursery located in Chapel Hill, NC, specializing in camellias and other Asian plants and known for its extensive collection and expertise in camellia cultivation.

7. **Johnson Nursery Corporation:** A wholesale grower in Willard, NC, producing a wide range of trees, shrubs, and perennials for the landscaping industry.

8. **Burpee's Seeds & Plants:** A well-known national seed and plant supplier that likely has operations or distribution in North Carolina.

9. **Van Wingerden International:** A large-scale greenhouse operation in Mills River, NC, producing annuals, perennials, and seasonal plants for wholesale distribution.

10. **Sage Hill Gardens:** A small, specialty nursery in Raleigh, NC, focusing on herbs, native plants, and pollinator-friendly species.

WORKPLACE COMPETENCIES:

1	Collaboration	Ability to work effectively with team members and clients to achieve shared goals in horticultural projects.
2	Problem-Solving	Identifying and resolving plant health or operational issues efficiently and creatively.
3	Technological Proficiency	Competence in using tools, machinery, and software specific to horticultural operations.
4	Project Management	Organizing tasks, resources, and schedules to complete projects on time and within budget.
5	Safety Awareness	Ensuring compliance with safety protocols to protect workers, plants, and the environment.

PERSONAL COMPETENCIES:

1	Attention to Detail	Observing and addressing minor changes in plant health or operational processes to ensure quality.
2	Adaptability	Flexibility to adjust to changing environmental conditions, client needs, and industry advancements.
3	Initiative	Proactively identifying opportunities for improvement or innovation in horticultural practices.
4	Communication	Effectively conveying ideas, instructions, and information to team members and clients.
5	Ethical Integrity	Upholding high moral standards and sustainable practices in all aspects of work.

KEY KNOWLEDGE, SKILLS, AND ABILITIES:

KNOWLEDGE	SKILLS	ABILITIES
Familiarity with plant biology, soil science, climate effects, and pest management.	Plant propagation, landscape design, and greenhouse management.	Physical stamina, attention to detail, and problem-solving.

RECOMMENDED HIGH SCHOOL COURSES TO PREPARE FOR A CAREER IN HORTICULTURE:

1	**Biology**	This course provides foundational knowledge on plant biology and ecosystems.
2	**Environmental Science**	This course teaches students about the impact of human activities on the environment, which is beneficial for sustainable horticultural practices.
3	**Agricultural Education**	This course focuses on basic agricultural techniques and practices, including plant care and soil management.
4	**Chemistry**	This course is essential for understanding fertilizers, pesticides, and soil nutrients.
5	**Business or Entrepreneurship**	This course helps develop skills to manage horticulture businesses or start a nursery or landscape company.

TOP 10 OCCUPATIONS IN HORTICULTURE:

Rank	Occupation	Education/Training	Average Wage
1	Horticulturist	Bachelor's degree in horticulture, plant science, or a related field.	$45,000–$60,000 per year
2	Greenhouse Manager	Bachelor's degree in horticulture or agriculture.	$50,000–$70,000 per year
3	Nursery Worker	High school diploma; on-the-job training.	$25,000–$35,000 per year
4	Landscape Designer	Bachelor's degree in landscape architecture or horticulture.	$55,000–$75,000 per year
5	Agricultural Extension Agent	Bachelor's degree in agricultural science or horticulture.	$45,000–$60,000 per year
6	Irrigation Specialist	High school diploma; irrigation systems certification.	$40,000–$55,000 per year
7	Floriculturist	Bachelor's degree in horticulture or botany.	$40,000–$60,000 per year
8	Arborist	Arborist certification.	$45,000–$65,000 per year
9	Plant Breeder	Master's degree or PhD in plant breeding or genetics.	$60,000–$80,000 per year
10	Farm Manager	Bachelor's degree in agriculture or horticulture.	$50,000–$70,000 per year

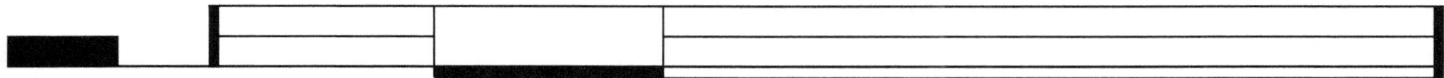

MY NOTES:

SECTION 16

CAREER PATHWAYS

NURSING

INDUSTRY OVERVIEW:

Picture this: North Carolina's nursing industry is like the superhero squad of healthcare. From the ER to your grandma's living room, nurses are out there saving lives, one bandage and pep talk at a time. With a cape made of scrubs and a superpower called "empathy," these everyday heroes are everywhere. Hospitals, clinics, schools—you name it. Whether it's keeping a tiny baby breathing in the NICU or convincing Mr. Johnson to *finally* take his meds, nurses are the MVPs of the medical world. So, if you've ever dreamed of being a real-life hero without the spandex, nursing could be your jam.

GROWTH PROJECTIONS:

The future for nursing in North Carolina is brighter than ever, with job opportunities expanding faster than your favorite coffee shop's drive-thru line. As healthcare needs surge due to an aging population and advancements in medical technology, the demand for skilled nurses is set to soar. By 2031, nursing jobs across the state are expected to grow significantly, with high demand in both urban hospitals and rural healthcare facilities. This growth offers job stability and countless pathways for career advancement, making nursing one of the most promising fields in North Carolina's workforce.

TYPES OF PRODUCTS AND SERVICES PRODUCED IN NURSING IN NORTH CAROLINA:

Patient care: Nurses deliver hands-on care by administering treatments, managing medications, and monitoring patient health to ensure optimal recovery and well-being.

Health education: Nurses educate patients and communities about disease prevention, healthy living, and managing chronic conditions to improve overall public health.

Specialized care: Nurses provide focused expertise in areas like pediatrics, oncology, and critical care to meet unique patient needs in diverse medical settings.

Support services: Nurses collaborate with healthcare teams to coordinate care, ensure safety, and improve patient outcomes across various environments.

Telehealth services: Nurses utilize digital platforms to offer remote consultations, monitor health conditions, and provide accessible care regardless of location.

NURSING COMPANIES IN NORTH CAROLINA:

1. **Duke University Health System:** One of the leading healthcare providers in North Carolina, offering a wide range of nursing roles across hospitals, clinics, and specialized care units.

2. **Advocate Health:** A company headquartered in Charlotte, NC—with a combined footprint across Alabama, Georgia, Illinois, North Carolina, South Carolina, and Wisconsin—and working to advance health equity and improve access and affordability for the people and communities it serves.

3. **UNC Health Care:** A statewide network of hospitals and clinics affiliated with the University of North Carolina, known for diverse nursing positions in teaching and research hospitals.

4. **Novant Health:** A four-state integrated network of physician clinics, outpatient centers, and hospitals across the Southeast US.

5. **WakeMed Health & Hospitals:** A Raleigh-based healthcare system that employs nurses in emergency care, pediatrics, and rehabilitation services.

6. **Cone Health:** A company located in Greensboro, NC, providing nursing jobs in acute care, home health, and community outreach programs.

7. **Mission Health (HCA Healthcare):** A company based in Asheville, NC, and Mission Health is part of HCA Healthcare, offering various nursing roles in critical care, oncology, and surgical units.

8. **UNC Health Blue Ridge:** A hospital anchoring the UNC Health Blue Ridge system of healthcare providers, located in Morganton, NC, and serving Burke County, NC.

9. **ECU Health:** A company serving eastern North Carolina and offering nursing careers in rural hospitals and specialized medical centers.

10. **VA North Carolina Health Care System:** A company providing nursing opportunities to serve veterans across multiple facilities, including hospitals and outpatient clinics in the state.

WORKPLACE COMPETENCIES:

1	Collaboration	Effectively working with interdisciplinary healthcare teams to ensure the best patient outcomes.
2	Time Management	Prioritizing tasks and managing workloads efficiently in fast-paced medical environments.
3	Problem-Solving	Assessing patient conditions and implementing effective, evidence-based solutions to medical challenges.
4	Adaptability	Responding quickly and effectively to changing circumstances, such as emergencies or evolving patient needs.
5	Attention to Detail	Ensuring accuracy in administering medications, documenting patient care, and monitoring health conditions.

PERSONAL COMPETENCIES:

1	Empathy	Demonstrating genuine care, understanding, and compassion toward patients and their families.
2	Resilience	Maintaining emotional stability and focus in high-pressure or emotionally taxing situations.
3	Dependability	Being reliable and consistent in delivering quality patient care and meeting responsibilities.
4	Continuous Learning	Staying current with medical advancements, technologies, and best practices through ongoing education.
5	Ethical Integrity	Upholding confidentiality, honesty, and professional ethics in all aspects of patient care and decision-making.

KEY KNOWLEDGE, SKILLS, AND ABILITIES

KNOWLEDGE:	SKILLS:	ABILITIES:
In-depth understanding of anatomy, physiology, and pharmacology; familiarity with healthcare regulations and patient safety standards.	Effective communication and interpersonal skills for patient and team interactions; proficiency in using medical technologies and electronic health records (EHR).	Ability to make decisions under pressure in high-stakes healthcare environments and adapt to varied patient needs and healthcare settings.

RECOMMENDED HIGH SCHOOL COURSES FOR A CAREER IN NURSING:

1	Biology	This course provides a strong foundation in human anatomy, physiology, and cellular biology, essential for understanding healthcare concepts.
2	Chemistry	This course teaches students the chemical principles behind medications, treatments, and the human body's biochemical processes.
3	Mathematics (Algebra and Statistics)	These courses help develop the problem-solving and analytical skills necessary for drug calculations, patient data interpretation, and research understanding.
4	Health Science or Anatomy & Physiology	These courses offer early exposure to healthcare concepts, including human body systems and medical terminology.
5	Psychology	This course helps students understand human behavior and mental health which are critical for patient care and communication.

TOP 10 OCCUPATIONS IN NURSING:

Rank	Occupation	Education/Training	Average Wage
1	**Registered Nurse (RN)**	Associate's degree in nursing or Bachelor of Science in Nursing; RN licensure.	$60,000–$95,000 per year
2	**Licensed Practical Nurse (LPN)**	Diploma or certificate from a state-approved nursing program; NCLEX-PN licensure (National Council Licensure Examination for Practical Nurses).	$40,000–$55,000 per year
3	**Nurse Practitioner (NP)**	Master of Science in Nursing or Doctor of Nursing Practice; national certification in a specialty.	$95,000–$135,000 per year
4	**Certified Nursing Assistant (CNA)**	Completion of a state-approved training program and certification exam.	$25,000–$35,000 per year
5	**Clinical Nurse Specialist (CNS)**	Master of Science in Nursing or Doctor of Nursing Practice with a clinical specialty focus; specialty certification.	$85,000–$120,000 per year
6	**Critical Care Nurse**	Bachelor of Science in Nursing; certification in critical care.	$75,000–$110,000 per year
7	**School Nurse**	Bachelor of Science in Nursing; state licensure and sometimes additional certification.	$45,000–$70,000 per year
8	**Public Health Nurse**	Bachelor of Science in Nursing; additional public health certification may be required.	$55,000–$80,000 per year
9	**Home Health Nurse**	Associate's degree in nursing or Bachelor of Science in Nursing; NCLEX-RN licensure and home health-specific training.	$50,000–$75,000 per year
10	**Nursing Educator**	Master of Science in Nursing or Doctor of Nursing Practice; teaching credentials or certification preferred.	$70,000–$100,000 per year

MY NOTES:

CAREER PATHWAYS

PUBLIC SAFETY & EMERGENCY MANAGEMENT

Explore
MY PATH

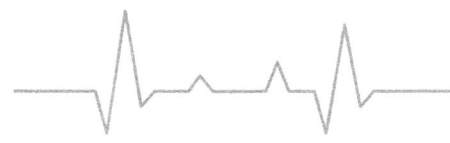

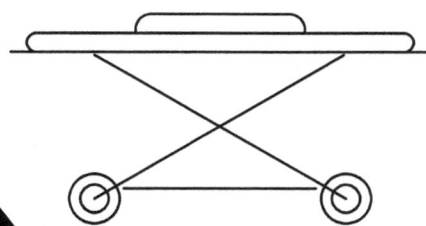

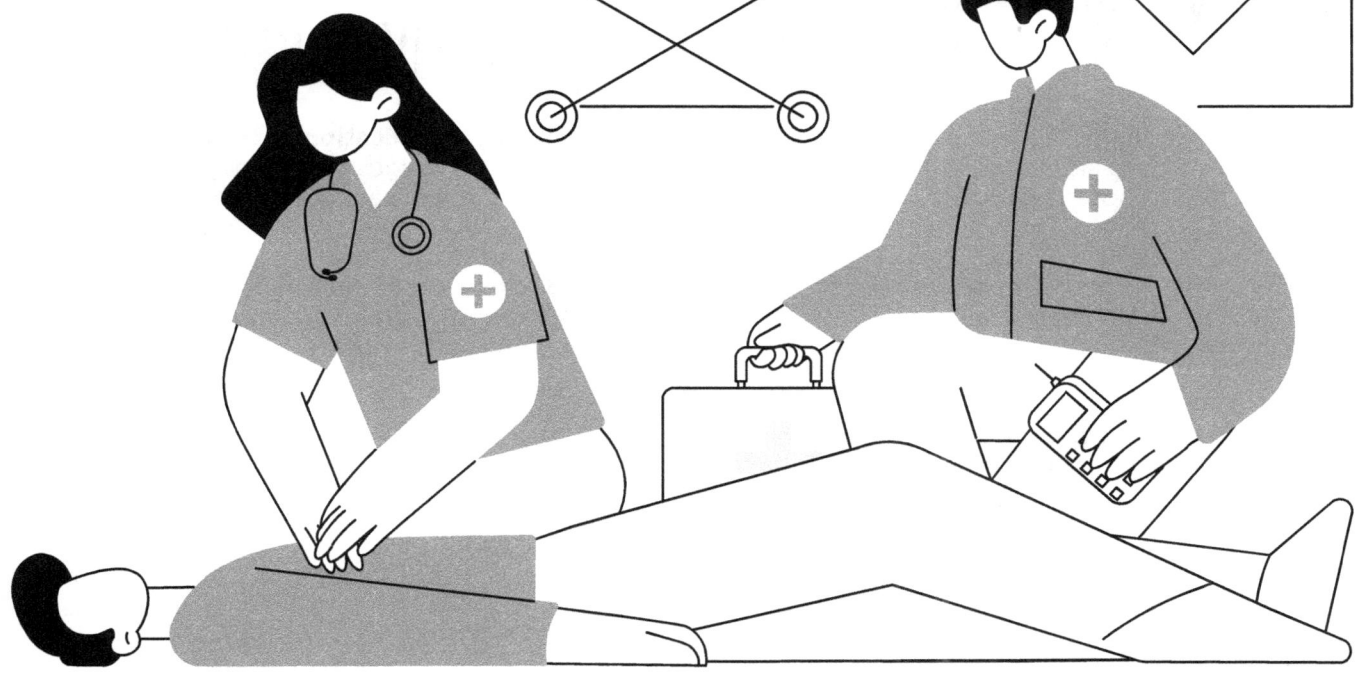

INDUSTRY OVERVIEW:

Hey there, future heroes! Ever thought about joining the ranks of North Carolina's public safety squad? We're talking cops, paramedics, firefighters, and disaster management pros—the real-life superheroes keeping our state safe and sound. As more people move in and Mother Nature throws us some curveballs (thanks, climate change), we need more awesome folks like you to step up. North Carolina's got everything from mountains to beaches, big cities to small towns, so there's never a dull moment in this line of work. It's all about protecting people, handling emergencies, and being ready for whatever comes our way.

GROWTH PROJECTIONS:

Good news, job hunters! The public safety and emergency management field in North Carolina is on the rise. We're talking a solid 5%–6% growth for law enforcement gigs over the next 10 years. But wait, there's more! If you're into calling the shots during crises, emergency management director roles are set to grow even faster at about 7%. Why the boost? People are all about community safety these days—plus, the state's gearing up for potential natural disasters like hurricanes and floods. So, if you're looking for a career that's not only rewarding but also in high demand, public safety just might be your ticket to making a real difference in the world.

TYPES OF PRODUCTS AND SERVICES PRODUCED IN PUBLIC SAFETY & EMERGENCY MANAGEMENT IN NORTH CAROLINA:

Emergency response plans: Detailed strategies for handling various crisis situations, tailored to specific regions and potential hazards.

Public alert systems: Technologies and protocols to rapidly disseminate critical information to residents during emergencies.

First responder training programs: Comprehensive courses designed to equip emergency personnel with the latest skills and knowledge.

Interoperable communication networks: Secure systems that allow various emergency agencies to effectively communicate during crises.

Search and rescue equipment: Specialized tools and vehicles designed to locate and extract individuals from dangerous situations.

PUBLIC SAFETY & EMERGENCY MANAGEMENT COMPANIES IN NORTH CAROLINA:

1. **North Carolina Department of Public Safety:** A state-level agency responsible for public safety, corrections, and emergency management across North Carolina.

2. **Charlotte-Mecklenburg Police Department:** The primary law enforcement agency serving Charlotte and unincorporated areas of Mecklenburg County, NC.

3. **Wake County Emergency Management:** An agency focused on coordinating emergency preparedness, response, and recovery efforts in Wake County, NC.

4. **Durham Police Department:** The main law enforcement agency for the city of Durham, NC, providing public safety services to the community.

5. **Guilford County Emergency Services:** An organization managing emergency medical services, fire services, and emergency management for Guilford County, NC.

6. **Fayetteville Police Department:** The primary law enforcement agency serving the city of Fayetteville, NC, ensuring public safety and order.

7. **New Hanover County Emergency Management:** An agency responsible for coordinating emergency preparedness and response efforts in New Hanover County, NC.

8. **Raleigh Police Department:** The main law enforcement agency for the city of Raleigh—North Carolina's capital—providing public safety services to residents.

9. **North Carolina Highway Patrol:** A state-level law enforcement agency primarily responsible for traffic safety and enforcement on North Carolina's highways.

10. **North Carolina Emergency Management:** A state-level agency coordinating emergency preparedness, response, and recovery efforts across North Carolina.

WORKPLACE COMPETENCIES:

1	Team Collaboration	Ability to work effectively within diverse teams, coordinating efforts during emergency response or routine public safety operations.
2	Problem-Solving	Skilled in analyzing complex situations to develop practical and timely solutions, especially in high-pressure scenarios.
3	Technological Proficiency	Competence in using advanced tools such as GIS mapping, emergency management software, and communication systems.
4	Adaptability	Flexibility to adjust to changing circumstances, new information, and unforeseen challenges during emergencies or daily tasks.
5	Attention to Detail	Precision in documentation, reporting, and following procedures to ensure compliance with laws and organizational policies.

PERSONAL COMPETENCIES:

1	Ethical Responsibility	Commitment to maintaining integrity, transparency, and professionalism in all actions and decisions.
2	Stress Management	Ability to remain calm and focused in high-stress situations, ensuring effective decision-making under pressure.
3	Leadership	Inspiring and guiding others, particularly during crises, to achieve goals and maintain morale.
4	Empathy	Understanding and addressing the needs of diverse populations, fostering trust and cooperation in public safety roles.
5	Continuous Learning	Dedication to staying updated with the latest techniques, technologies, and best practices in the field.

KEY KNOWLEDGE, SKILLS, AND ABILITIES:

KNOWLEDGE	SKILLS	ABILITIES
Familiarity with crisis management, disaster response protocols, and public safety laws; understanding of law enforcement procedures and community safety strategies.	Strong decision-making skills in high-pressure situations, crisis communication, conflict de-escalation, and proficiency with emergency management software and technologies.	Ability to remain calm under stress; high level of physical fitness and stamina; and problem-solving and rapid emergency assessment skills.

RECOMMENDED HIGH SCHOOL COURSES TO PREPARE FOR A CAREER IN PUBLIC SAFETY & EMERGENCY MANAGEMENT:

1	Introduction to Law and Public Safety	This course provides an overview of the legal system, public safety roles, and basic law enforcement principles.
2	Emergency Medical Responder	This course prepares students for emergency medical care, focusing on first aid, CPR, and basic EMT skills.
3	Criminal Justice	This course introduces students to the criminal justice system, criminal law, and corrections.
4	Physical Education	This course focuses on building the physical endurance and fitness required for physically demanding roles, such as firefighting or law enforcement.
5	Psychology	This course helps students understand human behavior, which is critical for roles involving crisis intervention and conflict resolution.

TOP 10 OCCUPATIONS IN PUBLIC SAFETY & EMERGENCY MANAGEMENT:

Rank	Occupation	Education/Training	Average Wage
1	Police Officer	Police academy; state certification; on-the-job training.	$55,000–$60,000 per year
2	Firefighter	Fire academy; certification; physical fitness requirements.	$45,000–$50,000 per year
3	Emergency Management Director	Bachelor's degree in emergency management or a related field.	$75,000–$85,000 per year
4	Paramedic/EMT	State-approved paramedic training and licensure.	$40,000–$45,000 per year
5	Criminal Investigator	Police academy; advanced investigative training.	$65,000–$75,000 per year
6	Correctional Officer	Training academy; state certification.	$40,000–$45,000 per year
7	Sheriff Deputy	Law enforcement training; firearm certification.	$50,000–$55,000 per year
8	911 Operator	Emergency communication systems certification.	$35,000–$40,000 per year
9	Search and Rescue Technician	Search and rescue operation training; EMT certification.	$45,000–$50,000 per year
10	Public Safety Director	Bachelor's or master's degree in public safety administration.	$90,000–$100,000 per year

MY NOTES:

CAREER PATHWAYS

RESIDENTIAL PROPERTY MANAGEMENT

Explore
MY PATH

INDUSTRY OVERVIEW:

Think of Residential Property Management as the engine that keeps apartment communities and rental homes running smoothly. It's about more than just collecting rent—it's also about welcoming new residents, ensuring buildings are safe and well maintained, addressing day-to-day challenges, and balancing budgets. Careers in this field can start with leasing apartments, fixing things as a maintenance tech, or supporting residents at the front desk and grow into managing entire communities, overseeing multiple properties, or even leading regional operations. It's a field in which strong people skills, problem-solving, and a little hands-on know-how come together, and the career ladder is clear: You can start at the ground floor and work your way up to leadership roles that pay six figures.

GROWTH PROJECTIONS:

So, what's the next big thing in North Carolina housing? Apartments, rentals, and build-to-rent neighborhoods, no doubt! In Charlotte and Raleigh, developers have been adding thousands of new units, and even though the market cooled a little in 2024, demand is still strong. That means steady jobs for leasing agents, maintenance techs, and community managers. According to the U.S. Bureau of Labor Statistics, the state's already home to nearly 7,890 property, real estate, and community association managers and more than 46,000 maintenance workers, and both fields are expected to keep growing through 2032. With big institutional investors moving into the Triangle and Charlotte ranking as one of the top markets for new apartment supply, it's safe to say property management isn't slowing down anytime soon. Pretty exciting if you're looking for a career with options, right?

TYPES OF PRODUCTS AND SERVICES PROVIDED IN RESIDENTIAL PROPERTY MANAGEMENT IN NORTH CAROLINA:

Multifamily Living: From sleek uptown high-rises in Charlotte to sprawling garden-style communities in Raleigh, multifamily apartments are the backbone of NC's rental market. With thousands of new units delivered each year, they create steady demand for leasing consultants, service techs, and property managers.

Affordable & Workforce Housing: Affordable housing is essential amid rising rents; authorities such as INLIVIAN need skilled managers to ensure compliance, conduct inspections, build partnerships, and advance workforce development with career pathways.

Build-to-Rent Neighborhoods: North Carolina is riding the national wave of single-family rental communities. These planned neighborhoods—complete with amenities like pools, playgrounds, and walking trails—need on-site teams to lease, maintain, and manage hundreds of homes.

Senior Living & Specialized Housing: As NC's population ages, demand for senior housing and managed care communities is climbing. These properties need managers who combine customer service with compliance and healthcare coordination.

RESIDENTIAL PROPERTY MANAGEMENT COMPANIES IN NORTH CAROLINA:

1. **Greater Charlotte Apartment Association (GCAA):** A leading industry organization supporting property management professionals across Charlotte and the surrounding region with training, networking, and advocacy.

2. **Drucker + Falk:** One of the nation's largest woman-owned property management firms with a major presence in North Carolina, managing multifamily, senior living, and commercial properties.

3. **RAM Partners, LLC:** A property management company operating numerous multifamily communities across the state, especially in the Triangle and Charlotte markets.

4. **Grubb Properties:** A Charlotte-based real estate investment and property management firm specializing in multifamily communities and mixed-use developments.

5. **Blue Ridge Companies:** Headquartered in High Point, NC, managing thousands of apartment units across the Carolinas and the Southeast.

6. **Ginkgo Residential:** A Charlotte-based firm focused on value-add multifamily property management, emphasizing sustainability and community development.

7. **Cortland:** A national property management company with a strong North Carolina footprint, including communities in Charlotte, Raleigh, and Durham.

8. **Bell Partners:** Headquartered in Greensboro, NC, Bell manages over 85,000 apartments nationwide, making it one of the largest multifamily management companies in the U.S.

9. **Lincoln Property Company (Southeast Division):** A national player with significant operations in North Carolina, managing both luxury and affordable apartment communities.

10. **INLIVIAN (Charlotte Housing Authority):** The public housing authority for Charlotte, managing affordable housing units, Housing Choice Vouchers, and community partnerships that connect residents with workforce opportunities.

WORKPLACE COMPETENCIES:

1	**Problem-Solving and Decision-Making**	Troubleshooting resident issues, maintenance requests, or leasing challenges and finding quick, practical solutions.
2	**Teamwork and Collaboration**	Building strong working relationships with contractors, vendors, and housing partners while staying open to feedback and collaboration.
3	**Communication**	Writing accurate service notes, professional emails, and compliance documentation to keep everyone on the same page.
4	**Time Management**	Balancing multiple responsibilities, leasing, budgeting, and maintenance calls, especially during peak leasing season or end-of-month deadlines.
5	**Adaptability and Flexibility**	Adjusting to new property management software, building systems, or market conditions with confidence.

PERSONAL COMPETENCIES:

1	**Professionalism and Reliability**	Showing up on time, prepared, and ready to support residents or teammates every day.
2	**Customer Service Mindset**	Listening with empathy and patience when residents raise concerns or complaints.
3	**Continuous Learning**	Staying current with NC's housing laws, fair housing regulations, and building technologies.
4	**Resilience and Stress Management**	Bouncing back from difficult resident interactions or challenging days with a professional attitude.
5	**Adaptability and Growth**	Being open to career mobility—moving from leasing into management or service into supervisory roles—as opportunities grow across North Carolina's expanding rental market.

KEY KNOWLEDGE, SKILLS, AND ABILITIES:

KNOWLEDGE	SKILLS	ABILITIES
Understanding federal, state, and local housing regulations to ensure compliance and protect both residents and property owners.	Accurately processing leases, inspecting apartments, and documenting maintenance work to meet compliance and quality standards.	Quickly assessing resident concerns or maintenance issues and finding effective, safe, and cost-efficient solutions.
Familiarity with budgets, rent rolls, occupancy reports, and revenue drivers that impact community performance.	Juggling tours, service requests, move-ins, and reports, especially in peak leasing season, while staying organized and efficient.	Using data, such as occupancy trends or service response times, to make decisions that boost resident satisfaction and property performance.
Knowing how to build strong resident relationships and maintain high satisfaction in competitive rental markets such as Charlotte and Raleigh.	Working seamlessly with leasing agents, service techs, and external vendors to keep communities running.	Explaining lease terms, writing service notes, or presenting updates to property owners in a clear and professional manner.

RECOMMENDED HIGH SCHOOL COURSES TO PREPARE FOR A CAREER IN RESIDENTIAL PROPERTY MANAGEMENT:

1	Business Studies	This course introduces basic business concepts, including management, marketing, and finance.
2	Accounting and Finance	This course provides foundational knowledge in financial literacy, accounting practices, and budget management.
3	Economics	This course helps students understand the principles of micro- and macroeconomics, which are essential in business decision-making.
4	Information Technology	This course familiarizes students with business software and data management tools, which are vital in today's tech-driven business world.
5	Leadership and Communication	This course helps students develop leadership skills, effective communication, and team collaboration techniques.

TOP 10 OCCUPATIONS IN RESIDENTIAL PROPERTY MANAGEMENT:

Rank	Occupation	Education/Training	Average Wage
1	**Leasing Consultant**	High school diploma or equivalent; customer service or sales experience preferred. NAAEI's *Certified Apartment Leasing Professional (CALP)* credential is valuable.	$37,000–$41,000 per year
2	**Assistant Property Manager**	High school diploma or associate's degree; training in property management software. Often promoted from leasing roles.	$45,000–$50,000 per year
3	**Property/ Community Manager**	Bachelor's degree in business, real estate, or related field helpful; *Certified Apartment Manager (CAM)* credential strongly recommended.	$61,000–$88,870 per year
4	**Regional Manager (Portfolio Manager)**	Bachelor's degree; years of property management experience; *Certified Apartment Portfolio Supervisor (CAPS)* credential preferred.	$90,000–$120,000 per year
5	**Maintenance Technician**	High school diploma or equivalent; technical training in HVAC, plumbing, or electrical; *Certificate for Apartment Maintenance Technicians (CAMT)* recommended.	$45,000–$53,000 per year
6	**Lead Maintenance Supervisor/Service Manager**	Technical certifications (EPA 608, OSHA, HVAC licenses); supervisory experience.	$55,000–$65,000 per year
7	**Groundskeeper/ Porter**	High school diploma or equivalent; on-the-job training.	$35,600–$40,000 per year
8	**Resident Services Coordinator**	Associate's or bachelor's degree in human services, social work, or related field; knowledge of housing programs.	$42,000–$50,000 per year
9	**Compliance Specialist (Affordable Housing)**	Bachelor's degree or equivalent experience; training in HUD/LIHTC compliance.	$50,000–$60,000 per year
10	**Facilities Manager (Large Sites/ Portfolios)**	Associate's or bachelor's degree in facilities management, construction, or engineering; strong technical background.	$65,000–$80,000 per year

MY NOTES:

CAREER PATHWAYS

SOFTWARE DEVELOPMENT

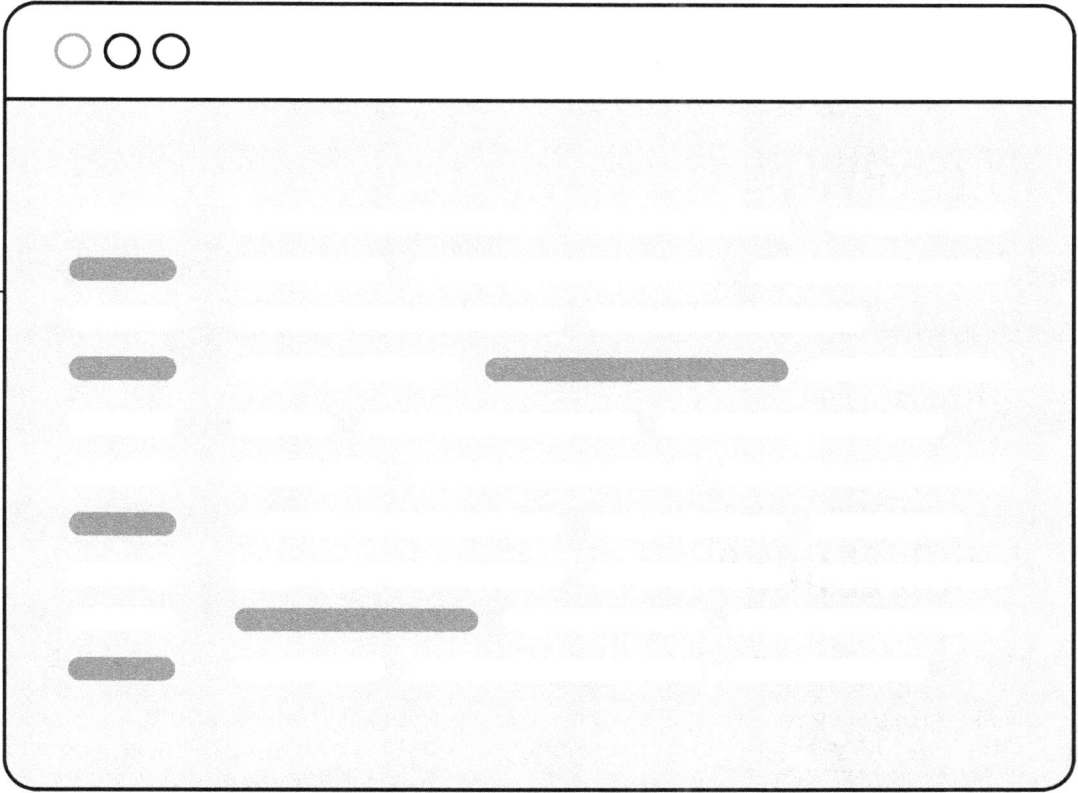

INDUSTRY OVERVIEW:

Let's talk about the software dev scene in North Carolina—it's on fire! The state's becoming a total tech hotspot, especially around the Research Triangle Park. Software's everywhere, from banking apps to health trackers to online shopping. And guess what? The demand for coding wizards is through the roof, all thanks to cool stuff like cloud computing, AI, and the technologies keeping our digital world safe from hackers. If you're into tech, there's a buffet of career options waiting for you—from crafting slick apps to crunching big data and playing digital bodyguard.

GROWTH PROJECTIONS:

Hold on to your keyboards because the future's looking bright! The software biz in North Carolina is set to grow like crazy—we're talking 8%–10% each year for the next 10 years. That's faster than you can say, "Hello, world!" Why? Everyone's hungry for cloud tech, mobile apps, and ways to make life easier with automation. Plus, North Carolina's totally got your back if you're dreaming of a tech career. The state's all about supporting tech businesses, and the schools here are churning out tech talent like there's no tomorrow. So, if you're thinking about jumping into the software world, North Carolina's the place to be!

TYPES OF PRODUCTS AND SERVICES PRODUCED IN SOFTWARE DEVELOPMENT IN NORTH CAROLINA:

Enterprise resource planning software: Integrated systems that manage core business processes for large organizations.

Financial technology (FinTech) solutions: Digital platforms and tools for banking, investment, and financial management.

Cybersecurity software: Tools and systems designed to protect digital assets and prevent data breaches.

Business intelligence and analytics tools: Software that helps companies analyze data and make informed decisions.

Educational technology: Digital learning platforms and tools for schools and online education.

SOFTWARE DEVELOPMENT COMPANIES IN NORTH CAROLINA:

1. **Red Hat (IBM):** A leading provider of open-source software solutions particularly known for its enterprise Linux distributions; acquired by IBM in 2019.

2. **SAS Institute:** A multinational developer of analytics software and a leader in business intelligence and data management solutions.

3. **Epic Games:** A video game and software developer—best known for creating the Unreal Engine and popular games like *Fortnite*—and a significant player in the digital distribution market with its Epic Games Store.

4. **Cisco Systems:** A global technology conglomerate that designs, manufactures, and sells networking hardware, software, and telecommunications equipment.

5. **Infosys:** An Indian multinational corporation providing business consulting, information technology, and outsourcing services.

6. **Bandwidth Inc:** A communications software company that provides a platform for voice, messaging, and emergency services, known for its APIs that allow businesses to add communication features to their applications.

7. **Pendo:** A software company that provides a product experience platform helping companies understand and guide their users.

8. **IBM:** A multinational technology company with a long history in computing, now focused on cloud computing, AI, and quantum computing among other areas.

9. **Relias:** A software company specializing in online training solutions for healthcare organizations, providing education and performance management tools to improve patient care and reduce risk.

10. **AvidXchange:** A FinTech company that provides accounts payable and payment automation solutions for midsize businesses, helping to streamline invoice and payment processes.

WORKPLACE COMPETENCIES:

1	Collaboration and Teamwork	Ability to work with cross-functional teams that include designers and engineers.
2	Adaptability	Continuous learning of new programming languages and tools as technology evolves.
3	Project Management	Understanding of project life cycles, from planning to testing and deployment.
4	Communication	Ability to clearly explain technical details to nontechnical stakeholders.

PERSONAL COMPETENCIES:

1	Attention to Detail	Precision in writing and reviewing code to avoid bugs and errors.
2	Problem-Solving	Aptitude for identifying and resolving technical challenges.
3	Lifelong Learning	Commitment to staying up-to-date with new tools, languages, and industry trends.
4	Time Management	Ability to manage deadlines and multitask in a fast-paced environment.

KEY KNOWLEDGE, SKILLS, AND ABILITIES:

KNOWLEDGE	SKILLS	ABILITIES
Familiarity with Agile, DevOps, and Scrum methodologies.	Proficiency in Java, Python, C++, and JavaScript.	Ability to solve complex issues and develop effective solutions.

RECOMMENDED HIGH SCHOOL COURSES TO PREPARE FOR A CAREER IN SOFTWARE DEVELOPMENT:

1	**Computer Science Principles**	This course introduces students to the fundamentals of computing, including programming, algorithms, and data.
2	**Mathematics (Algebra and Calculus)**	The math skills taught in these courses are essential for problem-solving and algorithm development in software.
3	**AP Computer Science A**	This course provides in-depth knowledge of Java programming and object-oriented design.
4	**Physics**	This course helps students develop logical thinking and problem-solving skills useful in programming.
5	**Web Development or Information Technology**	Hands-on courses in web development or IT fundamentals help students get practical exposure to coding and technology basics.

TOP 10 OCCUPATIONS IN SOFTWARE DEVELOPMENT:

Rank	Occupation	Education/Training	Average Wage
1	Software Developer	Bachelor's degree in computer science or a related field.	$100,000 per year
2	Full-Stack Developer	Bachelor's degree or coding bootcamp.	$110,000 per year
3	Data Scientist	Master's degree in data science or computer science.	$115,000 per year
4	DevOps Engineer	Bachelor's degree in IT or computer science.	$105,000 per year
5	Cloud Solutions Architect	Bachelor's or master's degree in computer science.	$130,000 per year
6	Front-End Developer	Bachelor's degree in web development.	$90,000 per year
7	Back-End Developer	Bachelor's degree in software engineering.	$95,000 per year
8	Software Quality Assurance Engineer	Bachelor's degree in computer science.	$80,000 per year
9	Cybersecurity Analyst	Bachelor's degree in cybersecurity or IT.	$95,000 per year
10	Machine Learning Engineer	Master's degree in computer science or a related field.	$120,000 per year

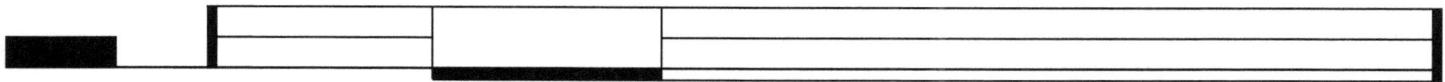

MY NOTES:

CAREER PATHWAYS

SPORTS & EVENT MARKETING

Explore
MY PATH

INDUSTRY OVERVIEW:

Hey, sports fans! North Carolina's sports and events marketing scene is seriously heating up. It's all about hyping and running the show for sports events, teams, star athletes, and cool entertainment stuff. We're talking everything from scoring big sponsorship deals to planning epic events, selling tickets, and getting fans pumped online. With a bunch of pro teams, college sports powerhouses, and awesome venues all over the state, there's a ton going on here. And get this—with social media and all things digital blowing up, teams and events are connecting with fans in wild new ways.

GROWTH PROJECTIONS:

Looking ahead, this industry's set to take off like a rocket. We're talking a solid 5%-7% growth each year. Why? People are pouring cash into fancy new sports facilities, esports are blowing up (yeah, gaming is a legit sport now), and—let's face it—North Carolina's college and pro teams are kind of a big deal. Plus, with everyone on social media these days and live streaming becoming the new normal, sports organizations are cashing in on these fresh ways to reach fans. It's a whole new ballgame out there, and the future's looking bright!

TYPES OF PRODUCTS AND SERVICES PRODUCED IN SPORTS & EVENT MARKETING IN NORTH CAROLINA:

Event ticketing services: Online and physical ticket sales platforms for sporting events and concerts.

Athlete endorsement management: Coordination and negotiation of deals between athletes and brands.

Event planning and logistics: Comprehensive services for organizing sports tournaments, races, and fan festivals.

Sports analytics and data services: Collection and analysis of performance and fan engagement metrics.

Virtual reality experiences: Immersive digital content allowing fans to remotely interact with teams and athletes.

SPORTS & EVENT MARKETING COMPANIES IN NORTH CAROLINA:

1. **Charlotte Sports Foundation:** A nonprofit organization that attracts, hosts, and manages major sporting events in the Charlotte area, known for organizing college football games and other high-profile sports events to boost the local economy and promote Charlotte, NC, as a sports destination.

2. **Wasserman Media Group:** A global sports marketing and talent management company representing athletes and brands across various sports, maintains connections to sports events and athletes in North Carolina.

3. **Visit NC:** The official tourism organization for North Carolina, promoting travel and tourism throughout the state, including for sports-related events and attractions.

4. **Tepper Sports and Entertainment:** A company founded by David Tepper that manages the Carolina Panthers (NFL) and Charlotte FC (MLS).

5. **North Carolina Courage:** A professional women's soccer team based in Cary, NC, competing in the National Women's Soccer League.

6. **Raleigh Convention Center:** A large convention and exhibition facility in downtown Raleigh, NC, that hosts sports-related events, conferences, and exhibitions.

7. **Hornets Sports & Entertainment (HSE):** The parent company of the Charlotte Hornets NBA team, managing the team's operations, business initiatives, and Spectrum Center events in Charlotte, North Carolina.

8. **IMG College:** A division of Endeavor specializing in collegiate sports marketing working with universities in North Carolina to manage various aspects of their athletic programs' marketing and media rights.

9. **Charlotte Regional Visitors Authority:** The official destination marketing organization for the Charlotte region, promoting tourism—including sports events—to drive economic impact and enhance quality of life in the area.

10. **Central Intercollegiate Athletic Association:** The oldest African American athletic conference in the US, based in Charlotte, NC, and organizing competitions for its member institutions, which are primarily historically Black colleges and universities in the Southeastern US.

WORKPLACE COMPETENCIES:

1	Collaboration and Teamwork	Working effectively with teams, vendors, athletes, and clients to ensure successful event marketing and execution.
2	Project Management	Overseeing marketing campaigns and managing timelines, budgets, and logistics for sports and entertainment events.
3	Customer Focus	Prioritizing fan engagement and customer satisfaction in all marketing efforts.
4	Technological Proficiency	Utilizing CRM tools, digital marketing platforms, and event management software.

PERSONAL COMPETENCIES:

1	Creativity and Innovation	Developing unique strategies to engage sports audiences and enhance the visibility of brands.
2	Adaptability	Flexibly responding to last-minute changes in event planning or marketing campaigns.
3	Ethics and Integrity	Conducting sponsorship and promotional deals with transparency and professionalism.
4	Problem-Solving	Quickly finding solutions to unexpected challenges during event marketing or sponsorship negotiations.

KEY KNOWLEDGE, SKILLS, AND ABILITIES:

KNOWLEDGE	SKILLS	ABILITIES
Understanding of sports marketing trends, digital and social media platforms, sponsorship agreements, and event management processes.	Strong communication; event coordination and social media marketing skills; and negotiation and customer engagement skills.	Ability to manage multiple projects, solve problems under pressure, adapt to evolving trends, and foster team collaboration.

RECOMMENDED HIGH SCHOOL COURSES TO PREPARE FOR A CAREER IN SPORTS & EVENT MARKETING:

1	Marketing Principles	This course introduces students to the fundamentals of marketing, including promotion, consumer behavior, and branding strategies.
2	Sports and Entertainment Marketing	This course focuses on the business aspects of the sports and entertainment industries, such as sponsorships, fan engagement, and promotions.
3	Digital Media and Communications	This course teaches essential skills in content creation, digital marketing, and social media management, all of which are critical in modern sports marketing.
4	Business Management	This course provides a foundation in leadership, organizational management, and project management, preparing students for the business side of event management.
5	Public Relations and Advertising	This course covers media relations, advertising strategies, and campaign management, which are important in promoting sports teams and events.

TOP 10 OCCUPATIONS IN SPORTS & EVENT MARKETING:

Rank	Occupation	Education/Training	Average Wage
1	Event Marketing Coordinator	Bachelor's degree in marketing, sports management, or a related field.	$50,000 per year
2	Sponsorship Manager	Bachelor's degree in marketing, business administration, or sports management.	$65,000 per year
3	Sports Marketing Manager	Bachelor's degree in marketing or sports management; MBA preferred.	$75,000 per year
4	Digital Content Specialist	Bachelor's degree in communications, digital media, or marketing.	$55,000 per year
5	Public Relations Specialist	Bachelor's degree in public relations, communications, or journalism.	$60,000 per year
6	Event Planner	Bachelor's degree in event management, hospitality, or business.	$48,000 per year
7	Social Media Manager	Bachelor's degree in digital marketing, communications, or a related field.	$52,000 per year
8	Brand Partnership Manager	Bachelor's degree in marketing, business, or sales; partnership development experience.	$70,000 per year
9	Ticket Sales Representative	Bachelor's degree in business, marketing, or sports management.	$45,000 per year + commission
10	Sports Analyst	Bachelor's degree in sports management, business, or data analytics.	$62,000 per year

MY NOTES:

CAREER PATHWAYS

LOCAL
GOVERNMENT

Explore
MY PATH

INDUSTRY OVERVIEW:

Local government in Charlotte-Mecklenburg is like your city's control center, handling essential services that keep daily life running smoothly. From emergency services and public schools to road maintenance and utilities, these organizations work to make the community function effectively and safely. Starting a career in local government can be rewarding, with opportunities in various departments like education, public safety, or community development. Many positions start at entry-level and offer paths to advance into leadership roles through experience and additional education, making it a solid career choice for those interested in public service.

GROWTH PROJECTIONS:

Basically, the government in Charlotte-Mecklenburg is like this huge operation that does pretty much everything around here. They're the ones making sure we have cops and firefighters, running our schools, and figuring out where new stuff gets built. It's pretty wild how much they handle. They've got people working on keeping us safe, making sure we don't get sick (all that public health stuff), running our schools, and planning where new buildings and parks will go. Without them, the whole city would be a total mess. So, there's a ton of different things you could do working for the county. You need to know your stuff and be good with people, since you'll be helping everyone who lives here. It's cool when you think about it—you could actually make a difference in your neighborhood!

TYPES OF SERVICES PROVIDED BY THE LOCAL GOVERNMENT IN CHARLOTTE-MECKLENBURG COUNTY:

Public safety: The City of Charlotte provides police, firefighters, and emergency responders 24/7 to protect citizens, respond to emergencies, and keep communities safe.

Infrastructure: The City of Charlotte builds and maintains the roads, bridges, sidewalks, and traffic systems that people use every day to get around safely.

Waste management: City of Charlotte workers collect trash, handle recycling, and process sewage to keep communities clean and prevent disease.

Public health: The Mecklenburg County Health Department protects communities by monitoring diseases, inspecting restaurants, providing vaccinations, and offering basic medical services to those in need.

Transportation: The City of Charlotte maintains public transit systems, including buses and trains, to help people get around the city affordably while reducing traffic and pollution.

LOCAL GOVERNMENT AGENCIES IN NORTH CAROLINA:

1. **Charlotte Water:** This City agency manages the public water supply, wastewater treatment, and stormwater services to ensure clean and safe water for residents.

2. **Charlotte Area Transit System (CATS):** This City agency manages public transportation services, including buses, streetcars, and the Lynx Light Rail system.

3. **Planning, Design & Development Department:** This City agency manages urban planning, zoning, land development, and building code enforcement to support sustainable growth.

4. **Housing & Neighborhood Services:** This City agency manages affordable housing initiatives, neighborhood revitalization programs, and tenant-landlord mediation services.

5. **Solid Waste Services:** This local agency manages waste collection, recycling programs, and landfill operations to promote environmental sustainability.

6. **Public Health Department:** This county agency manages health programs, disease prevention initiatives, maternal and child health services, and food safety inspections.

7. **Department of Social Services (DSS):** This County agency manages financial assistance programs, child welfare services, elder care support, and job training resources.

8. **Park and Recreation Department:** This local agency manages county parks, recreation centers, greenways, and public fitness programs to enhance community well-being.

9. **Land Use and Environmental Services Agency (LUESA):** This local agency manages environmental protection efforts, air and water quality programs, and building code enforcement.

10. **Criminal Justice Services:** This County agency manages pretrial services, offender rehabilitation programs, and criminal justice reform initiatives.

WORKPLACE COMPETENCIES:

1	Collaboration	Ability to work effectively in teams and cross-functional groups.
2	Critical Thinking	Ability to assess situations and make data-driven decisions.
3	Technology Proficiency	Competence in using business software and tools.
4	Client Focus	Maintaining a strong focus on customer satisfaction.
5	Time Management	Prioritizing tasks and efficiently managing multiple projects.

PERSONAL COMPETENCIES:

1	Integrity	Demonstrating ethical behavior and honesty in all business dealings.
2	Adaptability	Ability to adjust to changing market conditions and business needs.
3	Initiative	Taking proactive steps to achieve business goals.
4	Resilience	Handling challenges and setbacks with composure.
5	Continuous Learning	Staying updated on business trends, technology, and leadership practices.

KEY KNOWLEDGE, SKILLS, AND ABILITIES:

KNOWLEDGE	SKILLS	ABILITIES
Familiarity with public administration principles; government operations; and relevant laws, regulations, and policies.	Strong analytical and problem-solving abilities; effective communication and interpersonal skills; and proficiency in budgeting and financial management.	Ability to effectively lead and manage teams; capacity to develop and implement strategic plans; and aptitude for adapting to changing environments and policies.

RECOMMENDED HIGH SCHOOL COURSES TO PREPARE FOR A CAREER IN LOCAL GOVERNMENT:

1	**Business Studies**	This course introduces basic business concepts, including management, marketing, and finance.
2	**Accounting and Finance**	This course provides foundational knowledge in financial literacy, accounting practices, and budget management.
3	**Economics**	This course helps students understand the principles of micro- and macroeconomics, which are essential in business decision-making.
4	**Information Technology**	This course familiarizes students with business software and data management tools, which are vital in today's tech-driven business world.
5	**Leadership and Communication**	This course helps students develop leadership skills, effective communication, and team collaboration techniques.

TOP 10 OCCUPATIONS IN LOCAL GOVERNMENT:

Rank	Occupation	Education/Training	Average Wage
1	City Planner	Master's degree in urban planning or a related field; American Institute of Certified Planners license.	$75,000 per year
2	Police Officer	High school diploma; some departments require an associate's degree.	$65,000 per year
3	Public Health Nurse	Bachelor's degree in nursing.	$72,000 per year
4	Parks and Recreation Director	Bachelor's degree in recreation management or a related field.	$68,000 per year
5	Municipal Court Clerk	Associate's degree; some institutions require a bachelor's degree.	$45,000 per year
6	Civil Engineer	Bachelor's degree in civil engineering.	$85,000 per year
7	Emergency Dispatcher (911)	High school diploma.	$48,000 per year
8	Building Inspector	High school diploma; technical training and state certification in specific inspection areas.	$58,000 per year
9	Water Treatment Plant Operator	High school diploma; technical training.	$52,000 per year
10	Human Resources Manager	Bachelor's degree in human resources or a related field.	$78,000 per year

MY NOTES: